An Introduction to Object COBOL

E. Reed Doke
Bill C. Hardgrave

John Wiley & Sons, Inc.
New York • Chichester • Weinheim • Brisbane • Toronto • Singapore

Acquisitions Editor	Beth L Golub
Marketing Manager	Karen Allman
Production Editor	Kelly Tavares
Senior Designer	Dawn Stanley
Illustration Editor	Anna Melhorn

This book is printed on acid-free paper. ∞

Library of Congress Cataloging-in-Publication Data

Doke, E. Reed
    An introduction to object COBOL / E. Reed Doke, Bill C. Hardgrave.
        p.   cm.
    Includes index.
    ISBN 0-471-18346-6 (pbk. : alk . paper)
    1. COBOL (Computer program language) 2. Object-oriented
programming (Computer science)   I. Hardgrave, Bill C. II. Title.
QA76.73.C25D65   1998
  005.1 ' 17--dc21   97-13432
                                                     CIP

10 9 8 7 6 5 4 3 2 1

PREFACE

The Purpose of this Book

This book was written to provide you with an introduction to Object COBOL. It gives you the knowledge necessary to begin your understanding of how to design and develop information systems using this programming language. It is not intended as a comprehensive text for object-oriented (OO) technology or Object COBOL, or traditional procedural COBOL for that matter. We assume you have basic knowledge of traditional (non-OO) COBOL syntax. However, we have not assumed you are familiar with object-oriented concepts.

We have designed this book to be used by COBOL students in a university or technical school and by professional COBOL programmers. *A word of caution*: this book is an introductory text and is not intended to serve as a comprehensive technical reference for the object extensions described in the proposed 199X ANSI standard. We present only the basics.

We first describe OO in straightforward terms without the intensive vocabulary often encountered in other texts. Then, we go through the development of a relatively simple system using Object COBOL. The code is presented in detail and can be used by the reader. The companion diskette contains all of the examples from the book and can be executed.

We have included many programs, both procedural and object-oriented class programs, especially in Chapters 6 through 8, to demonstrate the ideas and concepts presented. With the exception of the Chapter 8 programs, all of the code was executed using the Micro Focus Personal COBOL for Windows system version 1.0. The system of programs presented in Chapter 8 was simply too large for the Personal COBOL software to execute.

A Word to Teachers of COBOL

We have designed and developed COBOL systems in industry and continue to teach COBOL programming classes at our respective universities. We have also participated in numerous discussions, with both other COBOL instructors and professional COBOL programmers from industry, about the best way to introduce OO concepts and Object COBOL into the existing information system (IS) curriculum. There appear to be two very diverse views on procedure. The first argues that OO and Object COBOL should be taught first, before the student's mind becomes cluttered with procedural techniques, such as programs and files. The contrasting view maintains that once students are familiar with the basic COBOL syntax, they can be exposed, gently, to the object-oriented paradigm and the related Object COBOL syntax.

We think both approaches have merit. We have been told that both approaches have met with success. Although in our classes we introduce OO toward the latter part of the advanced COBOL course, we believe it could be done earlier. The only difficulty is that in order for students to successfully write Object COBOL, they must be able to write some traditional COBOL, including data definition and procedural code. However, they do not necessarily need to be advanced COBOL students.

We would like to hear your ideas about this and learn of your experiences. Please let us know what has worked for you and what has not been so successful. You can contact us at our respective universities or through the publisher.

A Word to Practitioners

Today, in industry, as well as at many universities, a major controversy has arisen regarding the role of COBOL, especially Object COBOL, in future applications development. Some observers believe that COBOL is, at last, finally dead. They see COBOL as an obsolete mainframe batch tool whose demise has been too long delayed. At the other extreme, others, including the authors, believe that COBOL will continue to evolve and play a key role in systems development, especially with the implementation of the ANSI 199X COBOL standard. We develop this argument much more thoroughly in Chapters 3 and 4. However, we want to state at the beginning that if you are a COBOL developer, we strongly believe "you are in the right place at the right time." Your career will be greatly enhanced by learning about OO and Object COBOL.

How the Book is Organized

Chapter 1 begins with an overview of existing software development issues and presents reasons for adopting object-oriented technology. Chapter 2 continues with an introduction to OO concepts and presents these concepts in the context of a simple credit union application. Although all of the relevant OO concepts are presented along with realistic examples, this chapter is not vocabulary intensive; it is designed for users with no previous OO knowledge.

Chapter 3 presents reasons for studying Object COBOL and includes a brief comparison of Object COBOL with other OO development languages. Chapter 4 reviews the history of the COBOL language from its beginnings in 1960 through the proposed 199X ANSI standard.

Chapter 5 begins the specific discussion of the Object COBOL syntax. An object class from the credit union system is described, then a simple class program is developed and its methods are executed. Chapter 5 also introduces the idea of layered systems development in which a system is segmented into three components or layers: the user interface components, usually screens; the application processing (problem domain) components; and the data management components.

Chapter 6 introduces the concept of inheritance using the superclass from Chapter 5. Three new subclasses from the credit union are developed, and methods from all classes are executed.

Chapters 7 and 8 provide in-depth coverage of OO design and development. Chapter 7 develops data management classes for the credit union application using simple indexed files, whereas Chapter 8 presents screen interface classes using standard ACCEPT and DISPLAY techniques.

Chapter 9 recaps the OO and Object COBOL concepts presented in the earlier chapters and discusses how to continue your study of OO and Object COBOL. The chapter provides an overview of some OO programming concepts that are not covered in the previous chapters.

Each chapter includes review questions and exercises. In Chapters 5, 6, 7, and 8, the complete program listings are presented at the end of each chapter. Readers are encouraged to execute and experiment with the programs. We believe that working with the coding details of these programs will provide an important experience for those who want to learn about writing Object COBOL. In addition to reading about writing code, you need to actually do some writing. Good luck and have fun!

Acknowledgments

We want to thank the reviewers, especially Professor Donald Carr at Eastern Kentucky University, for their valuable and constructive feedback on the manuscript. Our special thanks also goes to Beth Lang Golub at John Wiley & Sons for her encouragement and support and to Lynn Grable at Southwest Missouri State University for her many hours of meticulous work in finalizing the manuscript.

E. Reed Doke
CIS Department
College of Business Administration
Southwest Missouri State University
Springfield, MO 65804
Internet: ERD836f@VMA.SMSU.EDU

Bill C. Hardgrave
CISQA Department
College of Business Administration
University of Arkansas
Fayetteville, AR 72701
Internet: WHARDGRA@COMP.UARK.EDU

Contents — An Introduction to Object COBOL

CHAPTER 1:

Why Study Object-Oriented Technology?

I have a cat named Trash. If I were trying to sell him (at least to a computer scientist), I would not stress that he is gentle to humans and is self-sufficient, living mostly on field mice. Rather, I would argue that he is object-oriented.
—Roger King (*My Cat Is Object-Oriented*)

A new era of software development is upon us. For over 20 years, software development has been based primarily on the structured development paradigm. During this period of time, we have seen information systems grow from simple recordkeeping systems to vast, sophisticated systems responsible for the daily operations and strategic importance of many companies. Today, companies cannot function without information systems. Information systems offer a way for companies to track transactions, plan for the future, and make important decisions. For many companies, information systems have provided a strategic competitive advantage. The infusion of information systems in organizations is so widespread and important that the study of information systems has become a requirement in almost all universities.

This new era has also ushered in new demands on information systems. Multimedia systems, incorporating video, sound, and graphics, are becoming widespread. Specialized system types, such as geographic information systems, require different approaches to development and storage. In addition, many of the systems that were written 15 to 20 years ago are about to outlive their usefulness. Years of maintenance on the systems have left the systems in a state of poor repair. Patches here and there have kept the systems going, but only barely. Now, as we approach the year 2000, the problems are going to intensify.

In this chapter, we will explore the nature of software development, some reasons for studying object-oriented technology (OOT), and the history of this technology. At the end of this chapter, you should have a good understanding why today's organizations need OOT to continue in the future.

"THE SOFTWARE CRISIS"

"If it ain't broke, why fix it?" Well, "it" is broke, or at least badly cracked—"it" being software development. Unfortunately, the systems development process is plagued with problems. For several years, the state of the software development industry has been affectionately labeled a *software crisis*. The main characteristics of the crisis include systems that (1) don't meet user requirements; (2) are overbudget; (3) are delivered late; and (4) are difficult to maintain. As indicated in Table 1.1, over 90% of systems in large organizations fail—at an average cost of $2,322,000! Failure, in this case, is indicated by a system that does not meet user requirements, is delivered late, or is overbudget. Failure rates for medium and small organizations aren't much lower.

Table 1.1 Software Failures

System Size	Average Cost	Average Failure Rate
Large	$2,322,000	91%
Medium	$1,331,000	84%
Small	$434,000	72%

Source: InfoWorld, February 6, 1995, p. 62.

The crisis has become such an integral part of the industry that we, as consumers of software, have grown to expect "imperfect" software. Just read any software "warranty." Recently, one of the authors received a software package that had with it a 20-page booklet entitled "Known Anomalies" (i.e., known problems). How many of us would buy a new car that came with a booklet of known problems? So, why are we willing to do so with software? It has become the culture. The business environment is so demanding and changes so rapidly that software companies are forced to release software before it has been thoroughly tested. A phrase often heard in software development companies is: "You can have it fast, cheap, and correct—pick any two." What a statement about software development! Users can either have a system fast and cheap, but one that does not meet requirements, or can adopt a system that meets requirements and is cheap but takes a long time to develop and deliver, or well, you get the picture. Products such as toasters and cars come with a warranty; software comes with a disclaimer.

Part of the problem with software development can be attributed to the demands from today's organizations. Today's systems are becoming increasingly more complex, utilizing PCs, client-server architectures, distributed processing, and graphical user interfaces (GUI). Today's projects are 10 times larger than those of the 1970s and early 1980s. Since the systems are 10 times larger, can't we just increase the number of people 10-fold? No, complexity grows exponentially, not linearly. For example, a 5,000-line program is much more difficult to write (i.e., more complex) than ten 500-line programs. (If you don't believe it, try it!) Thus, "keeping up" is not simply the case of adding more people (that would be linear growth). In today's environment, we must find a way of being more productive.

Demand for faster delivery of software is also growing in the competitive marketplace of today. Demand for systems is growing at an average of 12% per year, whereas the average annual productivity of software developers is increasing at only 8% per year. As shown in Figure 1.1, the "gap" between demand and the ability to keep up with demand (i.e., productivity) grows wider each year. What are the implications of demand growing faster than productivity? One implication is that there will be jobs for information systems personnel! A more severe implication is the growing *application backlog*. Typically, Fortune 1000 organizations experience a three to four-year backlog of information systems. This means that, on average, it takes three to four years to deliver a system to a user once the request for a system has been made. How useful is a system in three to four years

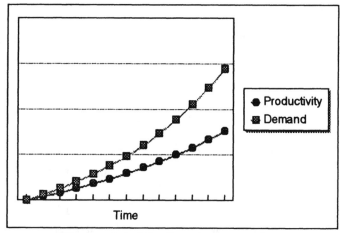

Figure 1.1 The Development Gap

AFTER it was requested? Business environments change, personnel change, business processes change; indeed, in today's environment of mergers and buyouts, the company may no longer be in business. This backlog is not acceptable. However, until we can increase productivity to pace, or surpass, demand, the backlog will continue to grow. Also, the three to four-year backlog is the backlog that can be measured. There is another backlog often referred to as the *invisible backlog*. When users realize that they may have to wait three to four years for a system, they quit asking. Thus, the invisible backlog indicates those systems that need to be developed but were never requested to be developed. The total backlog, including the invisible backlog, is estimated to be somewhere between six and eight years!

One barrier to increased productivity is the amount of effort spent on maintenance. It is estimated that an average company spends 70% or more of information system resources (i.e., money, man-hours) on maintenance (see Figure 1.2). It is further estimated that if we focused on new development only, it would take 15 years just to satisfy today's demands for information systems! Much of the blame for maintenance problems can be traced to systems written 20 or more years ago.

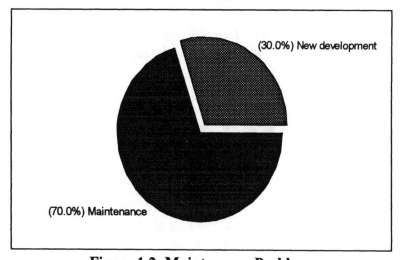

Figure 1.2 Maintenance Problems

At that time, millions of lines of unstructured code were written, and documentation was inadequate. In the next few years, the poor programming practices of yesteryear will be especially felt as we experience the *Year 2000 problem*. To save storage space, dates were stored in MM/DD/YY format—years are stored as only two digits. So far, this hasn't been a problem. However, in the year 2000 and beyond, any calculations involving years will be wrong. For example, in 1998 a person born in 1960 will be 38 years old (98 - 60 = 38) using today's systems; in the year 2000, the person will be minus 60 years old (00 - 60 = -60). Literally, billions of lines of code must be changed to avoid major problems on January 1, 2000. The problem goes beyond internal calculations: how many screens display four-digit years? How many reports print four-digit years? All of these will need to be changed. A survey of one company found the following: of 104 systems, 18 would fail in the year 2000. These 18 systems consist of 8,174 programs. It is estimated that major organizations will spend 35 to 40 cents per line of code to convert from a two-digit year to a four-digit year. For some large companies this translates into approximately $100 million.

Overall, current businesses face a dilemma: they are increasingly dependent on information systems, yet their ability to develop useful information systems is decreasing as the complexity of the information systems grows and the amount of information increases. Maintenance continues to devour the majority of the information system resources, which constrains the amount of effort spent on new development.

Is Object-Oriented Technology the Answer?

To help overcome many of the problems presented in the previous section, we need to build systems that are easy to maintain, flexible, scalable, and reusable. One possible solution is *object-oriented technology* (OOT). OOT is the name given to a new paradigm of software development based on the concept of an object, whereas *structured development* is based on the concept of business processes. It has been suggested that an organization's business processes change more than the data that are used to support those operations. An object's purpose is to represent the data and the procedures that have access to those data. (Don't worry if you don't understand the full meaning of OOT, objects, and so on. Chapter 2 will introduce and explain OOT concepts.) One of OOT's major advantages is the concept of reusability—objects act as independent entities that can be used to build a system.

During the past 30 years, hardware costs have decreased dramatically while software costs have continued to increase. Why? One reason hardware costs have been dropping has to do with the dramatic technological advances of recent years. However, hardware contains *standardized* components. Hardware is *constructed* from these components. In contrast, software is typically *crafted*. Each new system is designed and written with little benefit of reusable components. We need to build software like we do hardware: it needs to be assembled from standard components, and not handcrafted each time. One objective of OOT is to provide developers with the ability to *construct* software, taking advantage of *standardized* reusable components, instead of custom-developing all of the needed code. In other words, we want to *industrialize* software development.

Estimates obtained from various companies indicate that as much as 90% of all new code is unnecessary because the same or similar code has been created before. As software developers, we often adhere to the "not invented here" syndrome, which is interpreted as "if I didn't create it, it must not be good." We tend to create software code that has already been created. Think of the number of times you have rewritten header routines, or open and close routines, in COBOL. This is essentially reusable code. (Hopefully, you have learned to cut and paste from previous programs so that you can at least *reuse* some of your own code.) However, when placed in a development environment of hundreds of programmers, we have a tendency to use only our own code or to trust only our own code. OOT proliferates reusability. Objects become independent segments of a system that can be "plugged in" where needed.

The concept of an object as an independent entity not only facilitates reusability, but it also provides such benefits as flexibility and scalability. *Flexibility* (being able to change systems quickly and easily) and *scalability* (the system's ability to grow as the organizations grows) both affect maintenance. Maintenance, as we've seen earlier, is a major problem for organizations. As you proceed through this book, the improved maintenance of systems, due to OOT, will be obvious. (But just in case, we'll point instances out for you as we go.) If all of today's systems were based on OOT, we wouldn't have the Year 2000 problem, or at least the magnitude of the problem would be much smaller.

Is OOT a panacea for the software crisis? It probably isn't, but it may be the best available option. Organizations seem to think OOT may be the answer. According to a recent survey, only 3% of IT organizations were using OOT in 1994; 40% expected to be using it by 1997 and 80% by 2001. This indicates that companies are viewing OOT as a promising solution to software development problems.

In this book, we intend to illustrate the benefits of OOT via two avenues: the introduction of OOT concepts and the application of those concepts using an object-oriented programming language—Object COBOL. It is important to understand the concepts of OOT before learning how to design and develop OOT systems. Concepts are presented in Chapter 2.

Beginning with Chapter 5, Object COBOL is used to illustrate the development of an information system. But first let's get a little background on OOT.

History of Object-Oriented Technology

Because of all the recent attention being given to OOT, you may think it is a relatively new concept. Actually, OOT is more than 30 years old. The earliest object-oriented programming language (OOPL) was *SIMULA*, an acronym from SIMUlation LAnguage. It was developed in the mid-1960s in Norway. At the time, it was designed as a language to develop simulation models; however, it had many of the basic ideas contained in today's OOPLs. In 1971, *Smalltalk* was designed by Alan Kay and Dan Ingalls at Xerox Palo Alto Research Center (PARC) as the first pure OOPL. Incidentally,

Smalltalk also pioneered the development of today's graphical user interfaces. Smalltalk is called "pure" because everything in the language is an object. Smalltalk 80 (circa 1980) became the first commercial OOPL when Apple Computer offered the language with its Lisa computer in 1981. *C++*, currently the most popular OOPL, was introduced in 1985 as an extension of the popular C programming language.

In the 1980s object-oriented (OO) analysis and design began receiving attention based on the work of Booch, Coad, Rumbaugh, Shlaer and Mellor, Yourdon and others. In a paper published in 1982, Booch pioneered OO design as a method for Ada development. Other significant analysis and design methods introduced since this time include: Shlaer and Mellor; Coad and Yourdon; Objectory; object modeling technique (OMT); and responsibility-driven design.

In recent years (i.e., the 1990s), development methodologies designed to bring together OO programming, OO analysis, and OO design segments have been introduced. Booch has extended his original OO design to become a complete methodology. Other well-known OO methodologies are OMT and Martin and Odell's OO Information Engineering, among others. Table 1.2 summarizes the history of OOT.

Table 1.2   History of OOT

OO programming	mid 1960s
OO design	mid 1980s
OO analysis	late 1980s
OO methodologies	early 1990s

Today, the development and promotion of OO database management systems and OO CASE tools, as well as the availability of powerful OOPLs, promises to strengthen and hasten the move to OO development. In addition, the proliferation of GUI and the migration to client-server architectures provide additional motivation to employ OO. GUIs lend themselves quite well to OO development techniques.

Summary

This chapter has looked at the problems that we are currently facing in software development. As indicated, several problems exist—systems don't meet requirements, systems are overbudget or late, three to four-year backlogs exist, maintenance problems continue. All of these problems have contributed to the so-called software crisis. Unless something is done, the crisis will only get worse, especially when the year 2000 arrives. Recently, organizations have begun to investigate the use of OOT as an alternative to traditional development techniques. OOT offers the advantages of reusability, flexibility, scalability, and easier maintenance. The remainder of this book is devoted to the use of OOT as a method for developing systems.

KEY TERMS

Application backlog	Object-oriented technology	SIMULA
C++	Reuse	Smalltalk
Flexibility	Scalability	Structured development
Invisible backlog	Software crisis	Year 2000 problem

REVIEW QUESTIONS

1. What are the characteristics of the software crisis?

2. What is the average failure rate of information systems in organizations? What is the magnitude of this problem (i.e., in dollars)?

3. Why does an application backlog exist?

4. What is the Year 2000 problem?

5. Why does maintenance consume the majority of the IS budget?

6. Why (during the past 30 years) have software costs continued to rise while hardware costs continue to drop?

7. What are some benefits of OOT?

EXERCISES

1. Can today's organizations "survive" without OOT? If "yes," explain what an organization would have to do to effectively develop information systems without OOT. If "no," what will companies need to do to make the transition to OOT?

2. Do some companies require cutting-edge technology more than others?   Describe some companies that require cutting-edge technology and some that do not. Will this affect their decision to switch to OOT?

3. What could have been done to avoid the software crisis? Do you think software development will ever be free of the crisis?

4. Talk to some local companies about their application backlog. How large is their backlog? What are they doing to reduce the backlog?

5. Trace the history of OOT from its foundations through today. What did you find surprising about the history and origins of OOT? At what point in time did OOT really begin to be noticed by organizations? Are the concepts of "objects" found in other disciplines (e.g., engineering)?

BIBLIOGRAPHY

Booch, G. Object-Oriented Design with Applications. Benjamin-Cummings, 1991.

Brown, D. An Introduction to Object-Oriented Analysis. John Wiley & Sons, 1997.

Coad, P. Object Models: Strategies, Patterns, and Applications. Prentice-Hall, 1995.

Coad, P., and Yourdon, E. Object-Oriented Analysis. Yourdon Press, Prentice-Hall, 1991.

"Corporate IS Considers Object Plans." Computerworld, January 24, 1994: 61.

de Jager, P. "Doomsday," Computerworld. September 6, 1993: 105.

Katz, P., Kornatowski, J., Loomis, M., Shukla, A., and O'Brien, L. "Debatable Data." Computer Language. 10 (1), January 1993: 55–62.

Martin, J. and Odell, J. Object-Oriented Analysis and Design. Prentice-Hall, 1989.

Rumbaugh, J., et al. Object-Oriented Modeling and Design. Prentice-Hall, 1991.

Shlaer, S., and Mellor, S. J. Object Lifecycles: Modeling the World in States, Prentice-Hall, 1992.

Yourdon, E. Object-Oriented Systems Design: An Integrated Approach. Yourdon Press, Prentice-Hall, 1994.

CHAPTER 2:

Object-Oriented Concepts

Object-oriented programming will be in the 1980s what structured programming was in the 1970s. Everyone will be in favor of it. Every manufacturer will promote his products as supporting it. Every manager will pay lip service to it. Every programmer will practice it. And no one will know just what it is.
—Rentsch, 1982

The purpose of this chapter is to provide you with an introduction to basic object-oriented concepts. This is not, however, a vocabulary-intensive discussion. In fact, we will introduce you to only eight new terms:

Attribute	*Class*
Encapsulate	*Inheritance*
Instance	*Method*
Object	*Polymorphism*

These terms, plus the concepts they represent, are very adequate to provide the OO background you need to learn Object COBOL.

This chapter introduces a simple credit union application, which is the basis for examples throughout this and subsequent chapters. Then the systems development process is reviewed, and the motivation for using OO is discussed. Next, a brief history of OO is presented, after which OO concepts are introduced.

After studying this chapter, you will understand the primary differences between traditional and OO systems. In addition, you will be familiar with key OO terms and concepts.

The Credit Union System

The credit union operates in a small city and serves approximately 3,000 members. The members are primarily employees of a local manufacturing company. Employee dependents can also be members.

Each member is a customer and has at least one account. Three types of accounts are available: checking, savings, and loan. Furthermore, there are two types of loan accounts: automobile loans and home loans. A member can have several accounts. For example, a member could have two checking accounts, a savings account, as well as an automobile loan and a home loan. Each account will have a separate account number. Members are identified by their social security number.

Customer statements are produced each month and summarize all transactions for each account. The checking account does not pay interest. However, the savings accounts do pay interest, which is the same rate for all savings accounts. Interest is computed each month by multiplying the savings account interest rate by the average balance for the month. Each loan account is charged an interest rate, which was determined at the time the loan was established. The loan interest is computed by multiplying the loan's interest rate by the current loan balance. These computations are developed in more detail later.

OO Is The Same and OO Is Different

Some argue that OO is not all that different from traditional development methods, while others believe that OO is totally different. In reality, both positions have merit.

OO appears to be similar to traditional development methods because it employs some fundamental principles of good software engineering such as decomposing a problem into smaller, manageable modules and restricting data access. OO encourages modularization and *requires* restricted data access. However, we still must write code to define data, and we must write code to process that data. In OO terms, the data are called *attributes* and the code is called *methods*.

OO is quite different, however because an *object* becomes a system building block containing both data and code (attributes and methods)! In contrast, in a traditional system the data are contained in files, and we develop programs to access these files. However, an object owns and controls its data. The only way one object can access another object's data is to send that object a *message* requesting the data. The data are effectively hidden or *encapsulated*.

The only way then to access the data in an object is to send a message to that object. The message will invoke a method to carry out the desired process. An information system then becomes a set of *objects* that interact and collaborate by sending and receiving messages. In contrast, traditional systems consist of files and programs that access those files (see Figure 2.1).

Object-oriented programming languages (OOPLs) are also different. They use different syntax and terminology. Even Object COBOL, while retaining the familiar COBOL vocabulary, contains new syntax to accommodate the object extensions. OO analysis and design also use some unique terminology and notation. Significantly, the distinction between analysis and design becomes somewhat fuzzy in OO development.

In addition to OO differences, there are significant ongoing changes in the development environment, such as GUIs, client-server architecture, and the Internet. Although not directly a part of OO, these create new challenges for developers, which further complicates systems development.

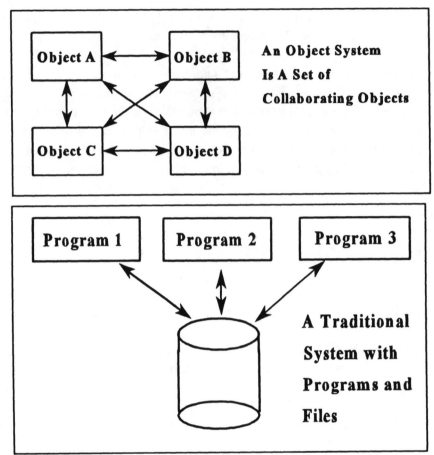

Figure 2.1 Contrasting Object and Traditional Systems

Finally, although OO has had some dramatic successes, it is not a panacea. Many of the design and development issues that we encounter in traditional development also exist in the world of OO. We can develop a *bad* system using the OO paradigm just as we can when using traditional structured techniques. OO only *enables* us to build better systems faster; it does not *assure* us that we will.

Software Objects Model Real-World Objects

When designing a software system using the OO methodology, we model ***real-world objects*** with ***software objects***. In Chapter 1, we said that the first OOPL was a simulation language (SIMULA). When we build software objects that represent real-world objects, we are actually *simulating* a part of the real world. One can argue that OO development is simply building a simulation model. Real-world objects are all around us. An employee, for example, is a real-world object. A student, a professor, and a customer are all examples of real-world objects. However, real-world objects are not limited to people.

Early in the study of our language, we learned that a noun was a person, place, or thing. A real-world object can be similarly specified. From the problem domain, we identify relevant people, places, and things. *People* can be customers, employees, members, students, and so forth. Examples of *places* are departments, regions, buildings, offices and rooms. *Things* can be tangible such as airplane, computer, statement, invoice, and transcript, or less tangible such as account, transaction, and reservation. Incidentally, one reason that OO works well with GUI applications is because the GUI windows and their components are *things* that can be modeled as objects. These GUI objects then interact with other system components.

Referring to our earlier credit union example, we note that we can identify several real-world objects: member, customer, teller, account, transaction, checking account, savings account, and loan account. Let's consider one real-world object from the example: a credit union customer. There are two characteristics of a customer we want to model: the things a customer *knows* and the things a customer *can do*. For example, a customer *knows* his or her name, address, phone number, and social security number. Things a customer *can do* include move (change addresses) and change phone number.

We can model this real-world customer object as a software object named Customer as shown in Figure 2.2. The Customer object will *know* its Name, Address, Telephone number, and Social Security Number. In addition, Customer will be able to *do things*: Change-Address and Change-Telephone-Number.

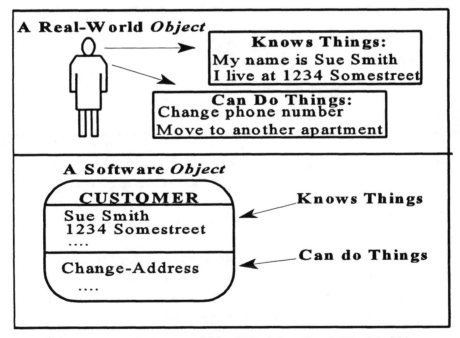

Figure 2.2 A Software *Object* Models a Real-World *Object*

The things Customer *knows* are called attributes and the things it *can do* are called methods. Our software object then has the following attributes and methods:

Attributes	Methods
Name	
Address	Change-Address
Phone-Number	Change-Phone-Number
Social-Security-Number	

In reality, our system will have many customers and, therefore, many objects. In fact, we will have one software object for each customer. If we have 3,000 real-world customers, then our system will have 3,000 customer software objects.

In OO, the correct term for each specific object is *Instance*. Therefore, in this example, we would have 3,000 instances of Customer. The group of customers is called a *Class*. Thus, we would have a single Customer Class with 3,000 instances. Figure 2.3 illustrates class and instance.

In an object system, an object's methods are executed when it receives a message, telling it, or more appropriately, asking it to invoke a particular method. Thus, if we want to change an address for a particular customer instance, we simply send that object a message requesting it to change the address to a new value. Such a message could appear as:

CHANGE-ADDRESS, Customer, Sue Smith, 1234 Somestreet

CHANGE-ADDRESS is the method, Customer is the class, Sue Smith is the instance, and the new address is 1234 Somestreet.

Class Relationships

Of course, the customer class will not accomplish very much acting alone; it needs to interact with other classes in order to do any processing. While developing the credit union system, we will model the other real-world objects that are needed for the system to be complete. Some of these classes we mentioned earlier are Account, Checking-Account, and Transaction. Can you name others?

In the real world, these objects interact. Customers deposit money to their accounts, make loan payments, and withdraw funds from savings accounts. Similarly, in our system which models the real-world system, these classes will have *relationships* with each other. For example, a customer will *have* an Account; deposits will be *made* to a Checking-Account; payments will be *made* for a Loan-Account.

In OO, there are three types of relationships between classes: *Is-a, Consists-of*, and *Association*. The Is-a relationship is the most important of these three. It occurs when we have a class that has subclasses which are special types of the class. To illustrate, in our system we have a class called

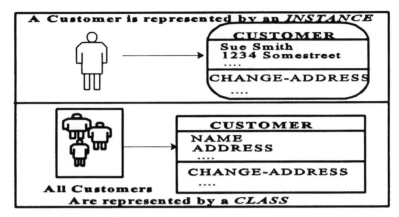

Figure 2.3   Class and Instance

Account. But we actually have three *types* of accounts: Checking-Account, Savings-Account, and Loan-Account. We can then say a Checking-Account Is-a Account, a Savings-Account Is-a Account, and Loan-Account Is-a Account. Another example is the *type* of Loan-Account. We will have a superclass called Loan-Account with subclasses Auto-Loan-Account and Home-Loan-Account, (see Figure 2.4). Account is the superclass of Checking-Account, Savings-Account, and Loan-Account. Conversely, Checking-Account, Savings-Account, and Loan-Account are all subclasses of Account.

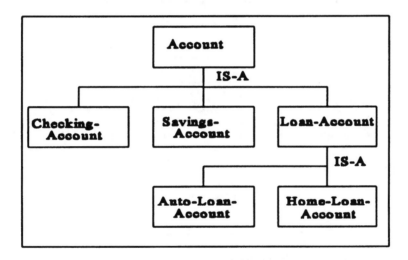

Figure 2.4   Is-a Relationships

Loan-Account is also a superclass of Auto-Loan-Account. Auto-Loan-Account and Home-Loan-Account are subclasses of Loan-Account. A *superclass* shares its attributes and methods with its subclass. A *subclass* uses the attributes and methods of its superclass.

Other examples will further illustrate the Is-a relationship. Tenured-Professor Is-a Professor and a Untenured-Professor Is-a Professor. Passenger-Airplane Is-a Airplane and Cargo-Airplane Is-a Airplane. Graduate-Student Is-a Student and Undergraduate-Student Is-a Student. Some of these relationships are shown in Figure 2.5.

Consists-of is a whole-part relationship. The whole Consists-of its component parts. For example, an Airplane Consists-of a Fuselage, Wings, Engines, and Landing Gear. A Computer Consists-of a

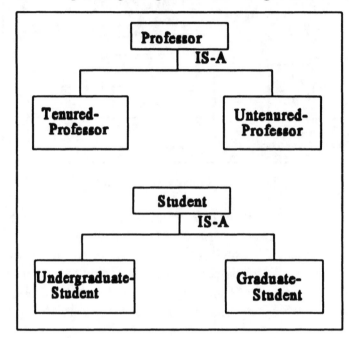

Figure 2.5 More IS-A Relationships

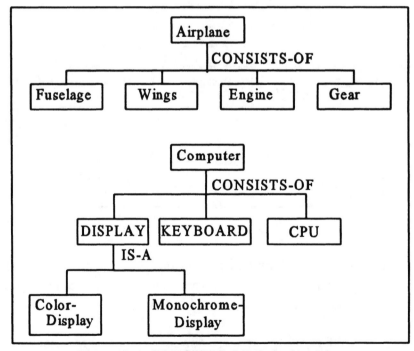

Figure 2.6 CONSISTS-OF Relationships

Display, a Keyboard, and a CPU. Figure 2.6 shows several Consists-of relationships. Notice that the figure actually contains both Consists-of and Is-a relationships. Computer Consists-of a

Display, a Keyboard, and a CPU, and Color-Display Is-a Display and Monochrome-Display Is-a Display.

The relationships between classes that are not Is-a or Consists-of are called Association. Earlier we mentioned that Customer will *have* an Account. At the University, a Professor *teaches* a Course and *conducts* Research-Project, Student *enrolls* in Course, and Customer *places* an Order. These are examples of Association relationships and are depicted in Figure 2.7.

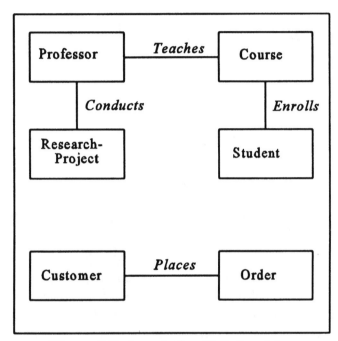

Figure 2.7 Association Relationships

Object Models

An *Object Model* is a graphical representation of classes and their relationships. The previous figures (2.4, 2.5, 2.6, and 2.7) that depicted Is-a, Consists-of and Association relationships are object models. Figure 2.8 is a more complete object model. It shows all three types of class relationships: Is-a, Consists-of, and Association.

Inheritance

Earlier, we said that the Is-a relationship was the most important of the three types of relationships. One reason it is important is that it provides for *inheritance*. Inheritance simply means that the attributes, methods, and relationships from a superclass are *inherited* by its subclasses. Inheritance is a form of reuse. Inherited attributes and methods are defined only in the superclass, yet they appear in all the subclasses.

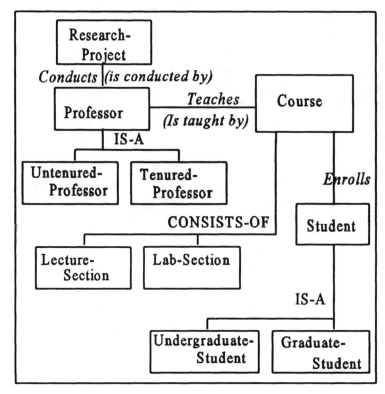

Figure 2.8   An Object Model

In the Is-a relationship, we will define some attributes and methods in the superclass and others in the subclasses.   Consider, for example, our Account superclass and the three subclasses: Checking-Account, Savings-Account, and Loan-Account.   There are attributes that will exist for all Accounts, regardless of their type.   For example, all Accounts will have an Account-Number and Current-Balance. In addition, all Accounts will be able to supply their balance through a method named Tell-Current-Balance.   These common attributes and methods will be defined in the superclass Account and will be inherited by all three subclasses.   Thus, each Checking-Account, Savings-Account, and Loan-Account will know its number and balance, and will be able to supply its balance, even though these attributes and method are defined *only in the superclass*, Account.

Some attributes and methods, however, are unique for the subclasses in this example.   For Checking-Account, we will want to track the Lowest-Balance which will be used for computing a service charge.   We will also want to have three methods for Checking-Account: Record-Check, Record-Deposit, and Compute-Svc-Chg.   The detailed logic for these methods will be developed in a later chapter.

Savings-Account will require two attributes: Interest-Earned and Average-Balance.   In addition, this class will have three methods: Record-Deposit, Record-Withdrawal, and Compute-Interest.

The Loan-Account class will have three attributes and two methods.   The attributes are Original-Balance, Interest-Rate, and Interest-Paid.   The methods are Record-Payment and Compute-Interest.

Figure 2.9 pictures these classes and their attributes and methods. Remember that the subclasses inherit the attributes and methods from the superclass, even though these are not explicitly shown in the subclasses. Now that you understand inheritance, we can provide a better definition for superclass and subclass. A superclass is any class from which other classes inherit attributes or methods. A subclass is any class that inherits from another class. Inheritance allows one particular class, such as Loan-Account, to be both a superclass and subclass. Loan-Account inherits from Account, which makes it a subclass. Loan-Account also has classes that inherit from it, such as Auto-Loan-Account.

Relationships are also inherited in the Is-a hierarchy (see Figure 2.8). The Professor class *teaches* Course and *conducts* Research-Project. The subclasses of Professor are Tenured-Professor and Untenured-Professor. These subclasses inherit the relationships of the superclass; therefore, Tenured-Professor and Untenured-Professor *teach* Course and *conduct* Research-Project.

Polymorphism

Polymorphism is a complicated-sounding word that is used for a very simple idea. Notice that both Savings-Account and Loan-Account have a method named Compute-Interest. Although these methods have the same name, they have very different logic. To illustrate, the Savings-Account Compute-Interest method will multiply the standard savings account interest rate by Average-

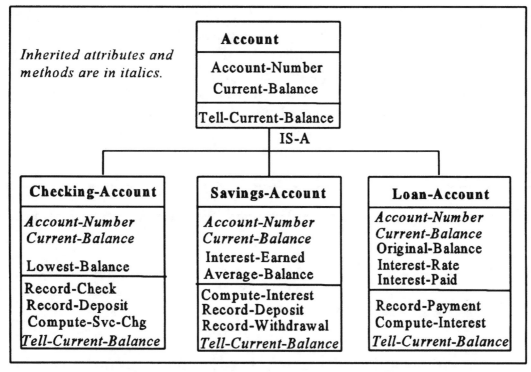

Figure 2.9 Inherited Attributes and Methods

Balance. However, the Loan-Account will multiply its individual Interest-Rate by the Current-Balance (which resides in the superclass, Account) to compute the month's loan interest.

Notice that both the Checking-Account and Savings-Account have methods named Record-Deposit. Again, these methods are similar and have the same name, but they do slightly different things. Can you guess how the Record-Deposit methods are different? Polymorphism exists when we use the same name for multiple methods that have different logic and therefore contain different code. Compute-Interest and Record-Deposit are both *polymorphic methods* in this example.

Advantages of Using Objects

We said earlier that OO promised to help us build better systems faster. You have seen that object classes have relationships and that the Is-a relationship provides for inheritance. You have also seen that objects interact by sending messages which invoke methods to provide system services.

There are numerous benefits of using objects, one of which is that software objects model real-world objects. It is more natural and an intuitive way of thinking. Using objects is much better than modeling real-world things and activities with files and programs. Our system design is a more realistic view of the real world. Another benefit of objects is data encapsulation. The data in an object is accessible only through that object's methods. This protects the data from corruption.

Inheritance provides several benefits. First, it obviously enables the reuse of attribute and method definition, thereby reducing redundancy. Second, inheritance facilitates maintenance. In our credit union system, if we need to add a new attribute to Account, the change does not need to be duplicated in the subclasses; it is automatically inherited. Also, to add a fourth type of Account, we simply define a new class containing only those attributes and methods that are unique to the new class, while allowing the common attributes and methods to be inherited.

Summary

This chapter has introduced basic object-oriented concepts. We began by describing a simple system for a credit union, and then we used this example to illustrate some OO concepts.

A software object models a real-world object: a person, place, or thing, tangible or intangible. Object systems consist of interacting and collaborating objects. These software objects interact by sending messages. Individual software objects are called instances. A group or category of objects is called a class.

The class contains data descriptions and code that executes to provide system functions. The data are called attributes, and the processing code is called methods. Methods are invoked when a message is received by the object. System services are provided by the methods.

The data in an object are encapsulated. It is accessible *only* by that object's methods. Other objects may request data through messages that invoke methods.

Object classes in a system have relationships. The three types of relationships are Is-a, Consists-of, and Association. The Is-a relationship provides for inheritance. Inheritance means the subclasses in an Is-a hierarchy inherit or copy the attributes, methods, and relationships from their superclass.

Polymorphism exists when we have two or more methods with the same name, but they do different things. Polymorphic methods have different logic and different code, although perhaps similar functions.

KEY TERMS

Attribute	**Is-a**	**Polymorphism**
Association	**Instance**	**Real-world object**
Class	**Message**	**Software object**
Consists-of	**Method**	**Subclass**
Encapsulate	**Object**	**Superclass**
Inheritance	**Object Model**	

REVIEW QUESTIONS

1.   How is OO similar to traditional development methods? How is it different?

2.   How does a software object differ from a real-world object?

3.   What is the difference between an instance and a class?

4.   What are the three types of relationships between classes?

5.   What is the relationship between inheritance and reuse?

6.   Can a class be both a superclass and a subclass?

7.   What are some benefits of inheritance?

EXERCISES

1. Given the following classes for a bank, draw the object model and speculate about attributes and methods. Add classes if you wish.

   Customer, Person, Business, Customer-Account, Savings-Account, Money-Market-Account, Auto-Loan-Account, Boat-Loan-Account.

2. Write brief descriptions of the following terms:
   - Object
   - Method
   - Class
   - Instance
   - Attribute
   - Encapsulate
   - Inheritance
   - Polymorphism

3. Does OOT guarantee that better systems will be developed? Why or why not?

4. Look around the room. Identify at least 10 real-world objects. For two of the objects, identify two attributes and two methods.

5. Using the objects identified in (4), identify and sketch an object model containing an Is-a relationship.

6. Using the objects identified in (4), identify and sketch an object model containing a Consists-of relationship.

7. Using the objects identified in (4), identify and sketch an object model containing an Association relationship.

8. Using the objects identified in (4), identify and sketch an object model that shows Is-a, Consists-of, and Association relationships. Can a particular class be involved in all three relationships? Give an example.

BIBLIOGRAPHY

Booch, G. Object-Oriented Design with Applications. Benjamin-Cummings, 1991.

Brown, D. An Introduction to Object-Oriented Analysis. John Wiley & Sons, 1997.

Coad, P. Object Models: Strategies, Patterns, and Applications. Prentice-Hall, 1995.

Coad, P., and Yourdon, E. Object-Oriented Analysis. Yourdon Press, Prentice-Hall, 1991.

Firesmith, D. G. Object-Oriented Requirements Analysis and Logical Design. John Wiley & Sons, 1993.

Jacobson, I. et al. Object-Oriented Software Engineering: A Use Case Driven Approach. Addison-Wesley, 1992.

Rumbaugh, J., et al. Object-Oriented Modeling and Design. Prentice-Hall, 1991.

Satzinger, J., and Orvik, T. Object-Oriented Approach: Concepts, Modeling, and Systems Development. Boyd & Fraser, 1996.

Taylor, D. A. Object-Oriented Technology: A Manager's Guide. Addison-Wesley, 1990.

Yourdon, E. Object-Oriented Systems Design: An Integrated Approach. Yourdon Press, Prentice-Hall, 1994.

CHAPTER 3:

Why Study Object COBOL?

The use of COBOL cripples the mind; its teaching should therefore, be regarded as a criminal offense.
—E.W. Dijkstra, May 1982

Many participants in the computing industry have decried and predicted the death of COBOL almost since its inception, as evidenced by the above quotation from one of the leaders in programming. However, not only is COBOL still "alive," it is by far the most dominant language in business.

COBOL's continued dominance in the field of programming languages can be attributed to three factors: (1) the number of programmers trained in COBOL; (2) the installed base of COBOL programs; and (3) COBOL's consistency as a business-oriented language. In addition, continuing improvements and enhancements to the language support its popularity.

In this chapter, we will expound on the reasons for COBOL's dominance. Among other things, we will look at the level of COBOL usage in companies which fuels the current and future demand for COBOL developers. We will also examine the increasing use of object-oriented (OO) technology and the growing demand for graphical user interfaces (GUI) and client-server architectures, together with their subsequent impact on COBOL. We also discuss the reasons for staying with COBOL.

After reading this chapter, you will understand the importance of COBOL in today's business world and have an appreciation for its importance in the businesses of tomorrow.

Current Demand for COBOL Developers

Currently, there are over 3 million COBOL programmers in the world. According to the Gartner Group, COBOL programmers represent 80% of all programmers in the world. COBOL is taught in many business information systems departments, thus continuing to produce COBOL programmers. A recent study reports that COBOL programming continues to be a highly demanded job skill—higher than any other language except 'C'. A different survey indicated that over 70% of all entry-level programming positions value knowledge of COBOL.

COBOL is the dominant programming language of the corporate world, with over 80% of *all* code written in COBOL. For the existing base of software, estimates range from 70 billion lines of COBOL code to over 200 billion. Although the estimates vary, it is fair to say that there are billions of lines of COBOL code.

Almost half of all development staffs in medium and large U.S. companies use COBOL as their primary language, and over 70% of all currently utilized business systems are written in COBOL. The amount of COBOL code in corporations is growing at approximately 15% per year, or, in other words, as much as 5 billion new lines of COBOL code per year!

The numbers are indeed staggering. It is obvious that COBOL is hardly dead or quickly dying; on the contrary, it is thriving. However, some changes on the horizon legitimately threaten COBOL's dominance. Two of the changes discussed here are the growth of object-oriented technology and the growing demand for graphical user interfaces and client-server architectures.

The Impact of OO on COBOL Developers

In moving to OO development, developers are responding to promises of faster, better, and less expensive development projects. Although, as we have said, OO is not new, it has recently become quite popular, in part because GUI environments lend themselves to OO techniques and in part because vendors have responded to the increasing demand for tools to develop systems faster, cheaper, and better.

The decision to move to OO, however, is closely coupled to the language selection decision. There are three types of OO languages to consider: (1) *native languages*; (2) *enhanced languages*; and (3) *visual languages*. Native languages, such as Smalltalk and Eiffel, originated from OO constructs and are considered "pure" OO languages. These languages "force" compliance of OO concepts on the programmer and support all of the major OO characteristics (such as polymorphism and inheritance). Enhanced languages, such as Object COBOL and C++, are third generation languages (3GL) that have been modified to include OO constructs. These languages provide programmers versed in the original 3GL a migration path to OO programming. Finally, visual languages, such as Visual Basic and PowerBuilder, are high-level languages tied to specific development environments. These languages are good for small systems but are not scalable to large, mission-critical, systems.

Given the large number of COBOL programmers and the billions of lines of COBOL code, it is unrealistic to think that COBOL will be abandoned. However, the growth of OO will require COBOL developers to adapt to the new paradigm. C++, currently the most widely used OO language, is difficult to learn quickly because of C++'s usage of cryptic mathematical, rather than business, notation. The proposed standard for ANSI-9X COBOL includes full object-oriented programming language extensions. Several vendors, including IBM, Micro Focus, and Hitachi, currently have Object COBOL compilers. Object COBOL provides the path needed by COBOL developers to move to OO.

The Impact of GUI and Client-Server on COBOL

COBOL is usually thought of as a mainframe-based, noninteractive programming language. For many applications, this may be true, but, COBOL is changing with the times. New development environments from IBM, Micro Focus, and others have moved COBOL into the GUI age. Now, COBOL can be used to create elaborate GUIs in a variety of environments, including Windows, OS/2, OSF/Motif, and even Web pages (html). Coupled with OO, the new COBOL development environment is ideal for constructing interactive business information systems.

For the past several years, companies have been moving to a client-server architecture (i.e., downsizing). The increased use of PCs and Unix environments left many wondering if COBOL could continue to be useful. Once again, the industry has responded by providing compilers and complete development environments useful for the client-server architecture. COBOL is available on a variety of platforms, including DOS, OS/2, VAX/MVS, and Unix.

Overall, COBOL is prepared to continue its dominance in business computing. Today's COBOL compilers include support for GUIs, networking, and nearly everything needed for business applications. The advent of GUI and the client-server architecture has only served to make COBOL more versatile and valuable.

Staying with COBOL?

For some time now, there has been a migration by companies from COBOL to C or C++. This is possibly the most serious mistake in IS history.
—Sitner, 1994

The three primary language options today are C++, Smalltalk, and Object COBOL. Each has its proponents and detractors, and valid reasons can be given both for and against each.

For example, C++ is a low-level and somewhat cryptic language with poor self-documenting features, a problem that raises legitimate quality and maintenance concerns. Smalltalk is a pure OO language, but important scalability and portability questions exist. Object COBOL meets the scalability and portability challenges.

Scalability indicates a language's ability to be useful for very large, as well as small, systems. COBOL is a proven language for large, mission-critical systems and is equally useful for small systems. Smalltalk and C++, on the other hand, have not proven to be useful for very large systems.

Portability signifies a language's ability to be used on many different computing platforms. C++ and Smalltalk are used primarily in the PC and Unix environments. Conversely, COBOL is available on many popular platforms, as indicated in the previous section. It is perhaps the most portable language available. COBOL is an industry standard language and is vendor-independent. The adherence to standards assure that it is portable (and scalable).

Although procedural COBOL has a solid track record, the object extensions are quite new and the ANSI standard is not expected to be published until 1998. In addition, viable vendor products are just now reaching the marketplace, which places early adopters of Object COBOL somewhat at risk. Table 3.1 summarizes a comparison of these languages.

Table 3.1 Comparing OOP Language Features

	Smalltalk	C++	Object COBOL
Inheritance	single	multiple	multiple
Encapsulation	total	limited	total
Polymorphism	yes	yes	yes
Classes as Objects	yes	no	yes
Persistent Objects	yes	no	yes
Dynamic Binding	yes	no	yes

Source: Saade and Wallace, 1995.

Adopting Object COBOL allows COBOL developers to leverage their existing language skills into the world of OO. The transition to the object paradigm is a nontrivial task, and coupling the transition difficulties with a new language adds needless obstacles to the transition.

The arguments for using Object COBOL sound familiar because they are essentially the same as those for adopting procedural COBOL. The language facilitates self-documentation, which results in highly maintainable code. Also, COBOL is standardized and easily meets the scalability and portability demands.

Migration from traditional to OO systems will take a long time and will require the coexistence of procedural legacy COBOL and Object COBOL. This coexistence may very well add complexity to the migration as developers are caught somewhere in between "purely" procedural and "purely" object development.

Finally, the COBOL language admittedly does have an image problem. It is often seen as an old-fashioned, extremely verbose, text-based development language limited to mainframe batch applications. Yet today's users expect GUI interfaces in a client-server architecture.

The truth is, COBOL is a dynamic, highly productive development tool whose syntax is understood by literally millions of applications developers. The dynamic nature of the language is clearly demonstrated by its continued evolution. Vendors continue to develop and promote COBOL-based tools that compete favorably in today's development climate, including GUI and client-server. Object COBOL is a logical continuation of this trend.

Future Demand for COBOL Developers

We don't know what the most popular application development language will look like in 15 years from now, but we know it will be called COBOL.
—Anonymous, 1993

*I am now convinced that my great-grandchildren, should they choose to become
programmers, will at least encounter—and may possibly use—some recognizable
descendent of COBOL.*
                                                        —R. Grehan, 1995

Obviously, many people believe that COBOL will continue to be a valid business programming
language; this is hardly debatable. However, whether it retains its dominance in an environment of
OO, GUI, and client-server is another question. We think it will. Several factors indicate that the
future demand for COBOL developers will be strong.

First, and most immediate, is the Year 2000 problem. As the year 2000 approaches, millions of lines
of COBOL code will need to be modified. Why? During the 1960s and 1970s, when disk space was
a major concern, programmers shortened years to two digits in order to conserve space. Now, as we
approach the millennium, the two-digit year will cause many problems to surface. For example, in
calculating the age of someone born in 1965, that person will be calculated as -65 years old (i.e., 00 -
65 = -65). This is but one of a plethora of problems that must be addressed before the end of the
century. All indicators suggest that the demand for COBOL programmers will increase between now
and 2000. Some believe that the most highly paid programmers in 1999 will be COBOL
programmers.

A second reason for the continued demand is the increasing stability of OO in industry and the use
of the three major OO languages - C++, Smalltalk, and Object COBOL. As mentioned in a previous
section, Object COBOL offers many advantages over Smalltalk and C++. In addition to those
previously discussed advantages, many companies will use Object COBOL as the path to migrate to
OO. Object COBOL has the advantage of reduced training needs and is compatible with existing
systems; therefore, it should be the OO development language of choice. In fact, the use of Object
COBOL (not including traditional COBOL) is expected to double in the next few years. Many major
corporations, such as Chase Manhattan Bank and Nationwide Insurance, have made the move to
Object COBOL. Thus, in the near future, demand for COBOL developers will be sustained.

Third, it has been suggested that high demand for COBOL programmers will continue because
existing COBOL systems require maintenance. According to Ed Yourdon (p. 16), "No matter how
bad the old legacy systems might be, they still carry out vital business functions. Many companies
can't justify the investment to replace 100 million COBOL statements with, say, 10 million Smalltalk
statements."

Summary

Almost since its inception, COBOL has been the dominant programming language for business
systems. Although many people believe that COBOL is "dying," industry indicators do not support
their contention. The current demand for COBOL programmers is high, and the current level of
COBOL usage in organizations is staggering. However, the recent growth of object-oriented
development, graphical user interfaces, and client-server architectures threatens the future of

COBOL. Industry has responded by providing the products necessary to develop GUI using COBOL and facilitate the use of COBOL in a client-server environment. In addition, a significant part of the proposed ANSI-9X COBOL standard is a response to the continued growth of object-oriented development in industry. Until very recently, the OO language choice was restricted to Smalltalk and C++, with C++ by far the most popular alternative. Now, the increasing availability of Object COBOL development products, plus the upcoming COBOL-9X standard, makes COBOL a viable language alternative.

Demand for COBOL developers will continue to be strong. In the near future, the Year 2000 problem will require an increase in the number of COBOL developers. In the long run, the increased use of Object COBOL and the required maintenance on existing COBOL programs should keep personnel demand high.

Key Terms

Enhanced language   **Portability**   **Visual language**
Native language   **Scalability**

Review Questions

1. What are the main reasons for COBOL's continued dominance as a programming language?

2. What are some threats to COBOL's dominance?

3. How widespread is the use of COBOL (i.e., number of programmers, lines of code)?

4. What are the three types of OO languages? Give an example of each.

5. What factors indicate strong future demand for COBOL programmers?

Exercises

1. Identify companies in your area which use COBOL as their primary development language. Ask a manager to give you his or her perceptions of the future of COBOL in 1, 5, 10, and 20 years.

2. Identify companies in your area that are developing GUI interfaces, using OO technology, or using a client/server architecture. What languages are they using? How do they see the future of COBOL? Is their perception different from what you found in (1)? If so, why do you think it is different?

BIBLIOGRAPHY

Adhikari, R. "Adopting OO Languages? Check Your Mindset at the Door" Software Magazine. 15 (12), November 1995: 49–50, 52–54, 58–59.

Appleby, D. "COBOL" Byte. 16 (10), October 1991: 129–131.

Clarke, D., and Garfunkel, J. "The Object-Oriented COBOL Model" Computer Standards & Interfaces. 15, 1993: 301–305.

Grehan, R. "Code Talk" Byte. 20 (12), December 1995: 216.

Hanna, M. "Is COBOL a Relic?" Software Magazine. 16 (4), April 1996: 61–69.

Harding, E. "OO COBOL—Too Late for the Party?" Software Magazine. 15 (4), April 1995: 25.

Hurwitz, J. "OO COBOL: Panacea or Paper Tiger? Object-Oriented COBOL" DBMS. 8 (9), August 1995: 12.

Katz, P., Kornatowski, J., Loomis, M., Shukla, A., and O'Brien, L. "Debatable Data" Computer Language. 10 (1), January 1993: 55–62.

Litecky, C., and Arnett, K. "A Longitudinal Study of the Most Wanted Skills in the MIS Job Market" 1994 National Proceedings of the Decision Sciences Institute. pp. 873–875.

McFarland, D. E. "COBOL Forges Ahead" Computerworld. June 5, 1995: 38.

Pinson, L. J. "Moving from COBOL to C and C++: OOP's Biggest Challenge" Journal of Object Oriented Programming. 7 (6), October 1994: 54–56.

Rabin, S. "Transitioning Information Systems COBOL Developers into Object COBOL Technicians" Object Magazine. January 1995: 71–75.

Saade, H., and Wallace, A. "COBOL '97: A Status Report" Dr. Dobb's Journal. 20 (10), October 1995: 52–54.

Sarath, P. "Object Oriented COBOL" Access to Wang. September 1995: 18–29.

Sitner, J. "Choose COBOL, not C, for Understanding Coding" Computerworld. May 30, 1994: 37.

Snyder, J. R. Encyclopedia of Computers. Macmillan, Vol. 1, 1992.

Sullivan, R. L. "Ghosts in the Machines" Forbes. 155 (13), June 19, 1995: 92.

Yourdon, E. "Micro Focus's Object-Oriented COBOL" <u>Application Development Strategies</u>. 7 (2), 1995: 1–16.

CHAPTER 4:

The Evolution of the COBOL Language

COBOL was conceived to solve "batch processing problems" in a sequentially ordered system.
—Clarke and Garfunkel, 1993

As discussed in Chapter 3, COBOL dominates the field of programming languages. For a language that was not supposed to be useful (according to many), it has continued to flourish over the years. Its continued dominance is even more surprising when we consider that by 1993 over 1000 programming languages had been introduced, yet COBOL continues to lead the pack.

COBOL was developed over 30 years ago out of a desire to have a true business-oriented language. At the time, COBOL's goals were simple: to be a language that was easily understood, self-documenting, and oriented toward business. Though simple, these goals were lofty because, at the time of COBOL's inception, there were no comparable languages. COBOL was developed at the right time and for the right reasons.

This chapter traces the history of COBOL from its inception through the next ANSI standard, COBOL-9X. COBOL has been updated several times in its short history, with each update aimed at improving an already excellent business programming language. After reading this chapter, you should know the history of the COBOL language and how each major release improved upon previous versions of the language.

Early COBOL (COBOL-60 through COBOL-68)

The first official version of COBOL was defined by the Conference on Data Systems Languages (CODASYL) committee. CODASYL was formed in 1959, largely at the urging of the Department of Defense (COBOL's goal was to save the government money in creating software). The committee consisted of government, industry, and academic leaders in computing technology. One of the original members was Grace Hopper, who became a driving force behind the development of COBOL. CODASYL published the first version of COBOL in April 1960, dubbed COBOL-60. This initial version contained only three divisions: environment, data, and procedure.

The next version of COBOL—COBOL-61—was introduced the following year. The major difference between COBOL-60 and COBOL-61 was the addition of the identification division. At this point, the four divisions of a COBOL program were set. The next standard, COBOL-65, added table handling.

In 1968, the COBOL standards committee of the American National Standards Institute (*ANSI*), known as X3.4, standardized the basic modules of the existing COBOL language. In 1970, ANSI approved the standard COBOL.

COBOL-74

COBOL-74 represented the next major release of the COBOL language. The most significant changes included improvements to table handling and sequential file access, and modifications to the random file access method and report writer. New features included a debug module, an *interprogram communication module* that made it possible to communicate with other programs, and a *general communication module* that provided the capability to interact with remote communication devices. In all, the COBOL-74 standard represented some 189 changes (modifications and additions) and 13 deletions from COBOL-68.

COBOL-85 and Addendum (Intrinsic Functions)

It would be another 11 years before the next major release of COBOL. In 1985, COBOL-85 was introduced. To date, this represented the most significant set of changes to the COBOL language—the most important of which was the adoption of structured programming techniques. Many in the industry were worried that the "new" COBOL would not be compatible with existing COBOL code. Resistance from the computing community was one reason why ANSI delayed approving the new COBOL. Although many features from COBOL-74 were eliminated to support structured programming, the majority of the existing language remained unchanged, and it did not lose its compatibility with older versions. In total, COBOL-85 introduced approximately 57 new reserved words. In addition to structured programming facilities, other major new features of COBOL-85 included (1) nested programs; (2) initialize statement; (3) access to substrings; (4) replace statement; (5) de-editing facilities; and (6) a more flexible form of variable-length records. COBOL-85 was also changed to support SQL and DB2. The 85 standard provided an estimated productivity boost of between 5 and 15% over COBOL-74.

In 1989, 42 new intrinsic functions were added to the standard in the form of an addendum. The next major revision for COBOL is scheduled for release in 199X (perhaps 1998?). This version incorporates the object-oriented programming (OOP) extensions, in addition to several other advances. Table 4.1 recaps the various versions of COBOL.

Table 4.1 COBOL Release History

YEAR	CHARACTERISTICS
1960	Initial release
1961	Added identification division
1965	Table handling added
1968	Seven modules defined and standardized
1974	Improved table handling, random access, and report writer plus debug module and subprogram facilities added
1985	Structured programming constructs added, plus DB2 and SQL support
1989	(ADDENDUM) 42 intrinsic functions added
199X	(Planned) OOP extensions plus dynamic array (table) allocation, bit and boolean data types

COBOL-9X: Object COBOL

The idea is to add just enough features to make COBOL a rich, OO model, while allowing COBOL shops and their existing skills to transition easily into the OO environment.
—Saade and Wallace, 1995

The extensions to the COBOL-85 standard, expected to be published in 199X (COBOL-9X), are designed to provide the language with full object-oriented programming language facilities as found in Smalltalk and C++, in addition to dynamic array (table) allocation, bit and boolean data types, and several miscellaneous features.

As with previous standards, COBOL-9X attempts to retain the familiarity of previous versions while adding the needed features and functionality. The OOPL extensions include one new verb, one new data type, plus new sections and headers to accommodate the definition of classes with their corresponding attributes and methods.

In Object COBOL, a COBOL program becomes a "class program" containing the method and attribute definition code for the class. Each class in an OO system is defined in a separate class program. Similar to Smalltalk, Object COBOL makes a distinction between class attributes and methods, and instance attributes and methods. The class definition code describes both inherited and inheritable attributes and methods.

The capability of writing nested programs was introduced in COBOL-85 and is extended in COBOL-9X. A class program can, and usually would, contain multiple method definitions for both the class and instance. Each of these method definitions appears to be "nested" within the class program. In addition, each method definition can contain its own data and procedure divisions.

Although ANSI has not released the official Object COBOL standards, several vendors have incorporated the anticipated standards into new releases of COBOL (see Table 4.2). Among the leaders in the Object COBOL movement are IBM and Micro Focus. Early use of these products indicates full compatibility with existing, procedural COBOL. Not only do these products include the Object COBOL extensions, but most also include necessary GUI and client-server features.

Table 4.2 Object COBOL Vendors

Name	Product
Hitachi Corp.	Object-Oriented COBOL
IBM Corp	Visual Age for COBOL, Object-Oriented COBOL
Micro Focus	Object COBOL Workbench, Visual Object COBOL
Netron, Inc.	Netron/Fusion
Computer Associates	Visual Relia COBOL
TechBridge Technology	TechBridge Builder

Summary

This chapter has traced the history of COBOL from inception through the proposed COBOL-9X (Object COBOL) standard. The next chapter will provide a detailed look at Object COBOL syntax.

Almost since its inception, COBOL has been the dominant programming language for business systems. However, the recent growth of object-oriented development threatens the future of COBOL. The proposed Object COBOL is in response to the continued growth of object-oriented development in industry.

Object COBOL vendors provide all of the tools today's developers demand. COBOL also diminishes the retraining hurdle while meeting important portability and scalability requirements.

Key Terms

ANSI
General communication module
Interprogram communication module

Review Questions

1. What was the original motivation for developing the COBOL language?

2. What was one reason for the long delay between the release of COBOL-74 and COBOL-85?

Exercises

1. Investigate one of the other leading OOP languages, such as C++ and Smalltalk. Why was the language originally developed (i.e., what was the purpose)? How popular is the language in business applications?

2. Access the Internet Web site WWW.COBOL.ORG. Investigate the information available through this source. Are there additional Internet resources for learning about Object COBOL? (*Hint:* search on the keyword COBOL and Object COBOL.)

BIBLIOGRAPHY

Adhikari, R. "Adopting OO Languages? Check Your Mind Set at the Door" <u>Software Magazine</u>. 15 (12), November 1995: 49–50, 52–54, 58–59.

Appleby, D. "COBOL" <u>Byte</u>. 16 (10), October 1991: 129–131.

Clarke, D., and Garfunkel, J. "The Object-Oriented COBOL Model" <u>Computer Standards & Interfaces</u>. 15, 1993: 301–305.

Feingold, C. <u>Fundamentals of Structured COBOL Programming</u>. 4th ed., Wm. C. Brown Publishers, 1983.

Grehan, R. "Object-Oriented COBOL" <u>Byte</u>. 19 (9), September 1994: 197–198.

Lauer, J., and Graf, D. "COBOL: Icon of the Past or Symbol of the Future?" <u>Journal of Computer Information Systems</u>. 34 (3), Spring 1994: 67–71.

Rabin, S. "ANSI 85: Understanding and Using the Latest COBOL Standard" <u>Computer Language</u>. 10 (3), March 1993: 67–68, 70, 72, 74, 76, 78.

Saade, H., and Wallace, A. "COBOL '97: A Status Report" <u>Dr. Dobb's Journal</u>. 20 (10), October 1995: 52–54.

Simkin, M. G. <u>Introduction to Computer Information Systems for Business</u>. Wm. C. Brown Publishers, 1987.

Snyder, J. R. <u>Encyclopedia of Computers</u>. Macmillan, Vol. 1, 1992.

Yourdon, E. "Micro Focus's Object-Oriented COBOL" <u>Application Development Strategies</u>. 7 (2), 1995: 1–16.

CHAPTER 5:

Fundamentals of Object COBOL

In the next four chapters (Chapters 5, 6, 7, and 8), we present the basics of Object COBOL using a small credit union system (introduced in Chapter 2). In these chapters, we will take a step-by-step, incremental approach to developing the system. As we develop the system, you will learn the Object COBOL syntax as well as techniques for writing object-oriented systems.

This chapter introduces you to the fundamentals of Object COBOL. You will become acquainted with its basic structure and syntax. You will also see how to use Object COBOL to define a class with attributes and methods. Then you will learn how to invoke the methods, and you will see how to create and access multiple instances of a class.

Also in this chapter, you will see the differences between class methods (also called factory methods) and instance methods. You will learn about the scope of data items in a class program, and you will be introduced to object interaction diagrams.

Figure 5.1 depicts one of the classes from the credit union system introduced in Chapter 2: Account. You will recall that Account had two attributes, *account-number* and *current-balance*, and one method, **TellCurrentBalance**. Here we have added a third attribute, *customer-ss-no,* and a new method, **OpenNewAccount**.

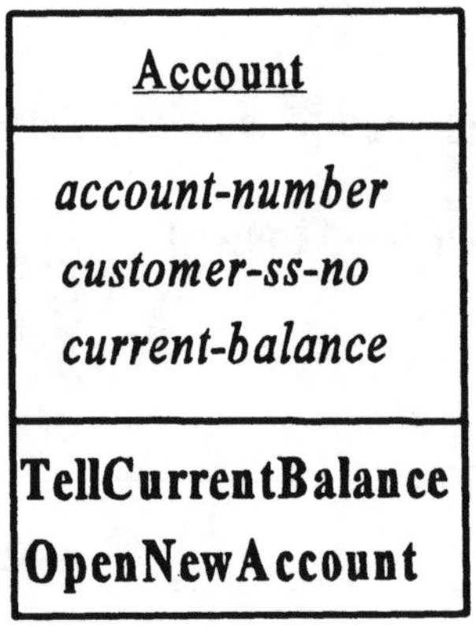

Account
account-number   *customer-ss-no*   *current-balance*
TellCurrentBalance   **OpenNewAccount**

Figure 5.1 The Account Class

In this chapter, we develop a class program for Account using Object COBOL. Then, we write a simple procedural COBOL program to invoke the methods in Account. After studying this chapter, you should be able to design and code a class program and write a procedural program to invoke methods in the class program. You will understand how OO techniques facilitate the design of layered systems, which are simpler and easier to maintain than traditional systems. We also introduce the concept of layered systems consisting of a user interface layer, an application processing (problem domain) layer, and a data management layer.

A Note About Notation

The following describes the notation conventions we have adopted here:

1. COBOL Verbs, Division and Section Headers, and Paragraph names are CAPITALIZED. Example: DATA DIVISION.

2. Method names are mixed case, boldface, no hyphens, with the first letter of each word capitalized. Example: **TellCurrentBalance**

3. Class names are mixed case with no hyphens, underlined, and with the first letter of each word capitalized. Examples: Account, LoanAccount.

4. Instance pointers use the class name with a prefix of "a" or "an." Example: anAccount

5. Attributes are lowercase and italicized with hyphens using appropriate suffixes. Example: *current-balance-ws*

A Class Program

Object COBOL enables us to write code to define a class, such as Account. In Object COBOL, this code is called a *class program* and it consists of data description entries for the attributes and code for the method definitions.

Figure 5.2 shows the Object COBOL class program for Account. As you review this code, you will see some familiar syntax such as division headers, level numbers, picture clauses, and MOVE statements. However, you will also notice there is some new syntax such as REPOSITORY and METHOD-ID. We will take a closer look at this syntax in the following paragraphs.

```
LINE                              Object COBOL Code
 1    IDENTIFICATION DIVISION.
 2    CLASS-ID. Account.
 3    ENVIRONMENT DIVISION.
 4    REPOSITORY.
 5        Account IS CLASS "Account".
 6    OBJECT.
 7    DATA DIVISION.

 8    WORKING-STORAGE SECTION.
 9  * Account attributes
10    01 account-number-ws     PIC 9(5).
11    01 customer-ss-no-ws      PIC 9(9).
12    01 current-balance-ws     PIC S9(5)V99.

13    METHOD-ID.  "TellCurrentBalance".
14    DATA DIVISION.
15    LINKAGE SECTION.
16    01 current-balance-ls     PIC S9(5)V99.
17    PROCEDURE DIVISION RETURNING current-balance-ls.
18        MOVE current-balance-ws to current-balance-ls
19        EXIT METHOD.
20    END METHOD.  "TellCurrentBalance".
21    END OBJECT.
22    END CLASS Account.
```

Figure 5.2 Account Class Program

The purpose of this class program is to define the <u>Account</u> class with its three attributes and two methods. (*Note*: Only one method is defined in Figure 5.2.) The attributes are defined in lines 10 through 12 as shown below.

```
 8      WORKING-STORAGE SECTION.
 9    * Account attributes
10      01 account-number-ws     PIC 9(5).
11      01 customer-ss-no-ws      PIC 9(9).
12      01 current-balance-ws     PIC S9(5)V99.
```

You will notice that the code used to define the attributes *account-number-ws*, *customer-ss-no-ws*, and *current-balance-ws* uses familiar procedural COBOL syntax contained in the WORKING-STORAGE SECTION of the DATA DIVISION.

The method, **TellCurrentBalance,** is defined in lines 13 through 20 shown below.

```
13    METHOD-ID.  "TellCurrentBalance".
14    DATA DIVISION.
15    LINKAGE SECTION.
16    01 current-balance-ls          PIC S9(5)V99.
17    PROCEDURE DIVISION    RETURNING  current-balance-ls.
18       MOVE current-balance-ws TO current-balance-ls
19       EXIT METHOD.
20    END METHOD.  "TellCurrentBalance".
```

Let's look more closely at the method definition code because it contains some new syntax. In some ways, a method resembles a program with its own DATA and PROCEDURE divisions. Line 13 contains a METHOD-ID clause that indicates the beginning of the method and also names the method, **TellCurrentBalance**. Similarly, line 20 is an END METHOD clause that is a scope terminator indicating the last line of the method. Although the method's DATA DIVISION, lines 14–16, can contain any valid section headers such as WORKING-STORAGE SECTION, LINKAGE SECTION and REPORT SECTION, this example requires only a LINKAGE SECTION.

Actually, this class program has two data divisions. The first, at line 7, which contains the attribute definitions, may be used by any method in this class. However, the second data division at line 14 contains data definitions only for the method **TellCurrentBalance**. We will discuss this idea called "scope" in more detail later in the chapter.

In procedural COBOL, we use the CALL statement to invoke the execution of a subprogram. We also pass data to a subprogram and receive data back from the subprogram. The LINKAGE SECTION is used by a subprogram both to receive and to return data from a calling program. Similarly, in a method, the Linkage Section is used to receive data from the invoking object and return data to the invoking object. In the Account example, **TellCurrentBalance** uses the LINKAGE SECTION entry, *current-balance-ls*, at line 16 to return the current balance of the account to the invoking object.

The PROCEDURE DIVISION in the **TellCurrentBalance** method is very brief, but then, its only purpose is to supply a value to the invoking object. Line 18 provides the value of *current-balance* by moving *current-balance-ws* in the WORKING-STORAGE SECTION to *current-balance-ls* in the LINKAGE SECTION. Remember that the LINKAGE SECTION is used to pass data between objects. In this example, the data being passed to the invoking object is the current balance for the Account, which is contained in the attribute *current-balance-ws* defined at line 12 in the class program.

INVOKING a Method

In an object-oriented system, objects interact by sending messages that invoke methods. These methods provide system services. However, unlike a system consisting of procedural programs, nothing happens in an OO system until a method is invoked. In our example, the method **TellCurrentBalance** will be invoked to supply an account balance. We will write a simple procedural program to invoke this method. Figure 5.3 shows this program, named the *Driver Program* because it "drives" the system.

LINE	Object COBOL Code

```
1    IDENTIFICATION DIVISION.
2    PROGRAM-ID. Driver.
3    ENVIRONMENT DIVISION.
4    REPOSITORY.
5        Account IS CLASS "Account".
6    DATA DIVISION.

7    WORKING-STORAGE SECTION.
8    01 anAccount        USAGE IS OBJECT REFERENCE.
9    01 current-balance-ws    PIC S9(5)V99.

10   PROCEDURE DIVISION
11       INVOKE anAccount "TellCurrentBalance"
12           RETURNING current-balance-ws.
13       DISPLAY "The Current Balance is:",current-balance-ws
14       STOP RUN.
```

Figure 5.3 A Procedural Program to INVOKE TellCurrentBalance

This driver program contains three new statements. First, line 5 tells the COBOL compiler the name of the class program we will be accessing: Account. Second, line 8 contains a new data type, Object Reference. This data item, anAccount, is actually a pointer that points to a specific Account instance. Remember that we can have literally thousands of accounts. anAccount will contain a pointer to the account we want to access.

The third new statement, INVOKE, at line 11 sends a message to the instance of Account, requesting it to execute the method **TellCurrentBalance**. In this example, let's assume we already have an account instance for account number 1 with a balance of 678.90.

When the driver program is executed, five steps occur:

1. Line 11 in driver is executed, which transfers control to the **TellCurrentBalance** method at line 17 in the Account class program (see Figure 5.2).

2. Line 18 in Account is executed, which moves the current balance of the account to the current balance data element in the linkage section.

3. Line 19 in <u>Account</u> is executed, which returns execution to line 13 in the driver program.

4. Line 13 in driver is executed, which displays the contents of *current-balance-ws*.

5. Line 14 in driver is executed, which terminates the program.

Figure 5.4 graphically illustrates these five steps. Use of the driver and class programs clearly demonstrates the concepts of client-server architecture. In this case, the client (i.e., driver program) invokes the server (i.e., class programs) to perform a function. The client clearly does not know how the server satisfies the request; it only knows the message to send to achieve the desired response. This simple example illustrates how easily OO systems facilitate a client-server environment.

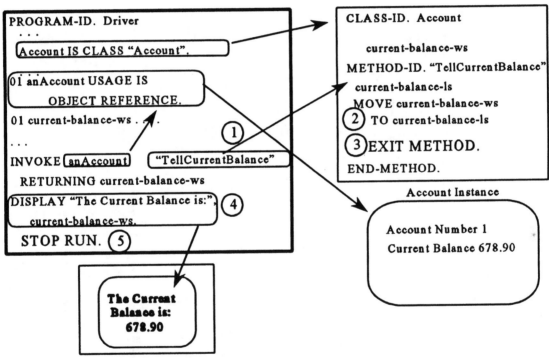

Figure 5.4   The Execution of TellCurrentBalance

Object Interaction Diagrams

The step-by-step description of the execution of **TellCurrentBalance** is adequate for simple interactions between a program, such as Driver, and an object, or between two objects. However, for more complex interactions, especially interactions involving several objects, an *object interaction diagram* is a much better tool to describe message flow than a step-by-step narrative. The object interaction diagram is a simple tool that does an excellent job of showing message flow between objects.

Various forms of the object interaction diagram have been proposed. These forms have been called module diagrams (Booch), event trace models (Rumbaugh), and interaction diagrams (Jacobson). Here, we will use the term object interaction diagram (OID). The OID uses simple notation as shown in Figure 5.5.

We know that in an object system, objects interact to provide system services. They interact by sending messages back and forth. In Object COBOL we send a message using the INVOKE verb.

Figure 5.6 shows an OID for our previous **TellCurrentBalance** example. At step 1 driver invokes the **TellCurrentBalance** method in <u>Account</u>. At step 2 <u>Account</u> returns the parameter current-balance.

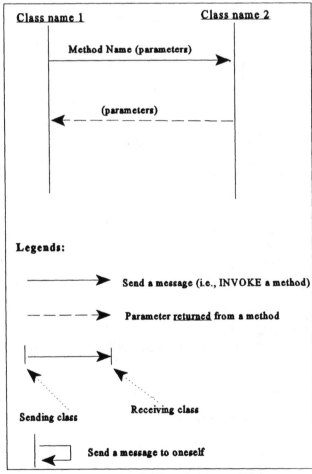

**Figure 5.5   Object Interaction
Diagram Notation**

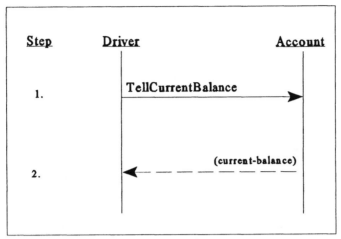

**Figure 5.6   An Object Interaction Diagram
for TellCurrentBalance**

Factory Methods and Instance Methods

Class programs may actually have two types of methods: *factory methods*, also called *class methods*, and *instance methods*. An instance method is used to do processing for individual instances (individual accounts in our example). A factory method handles the processing for a group of objects (all accounts in our example). In general, factory methods provide services for the class as a whole, while instance methods provide services for an instance. For example, **TellCurrentBalance** is an instance method because it tells the balance for a specific account. On the other hand, **OpenNewAccount,** described in the next section, is a factory method because it is invoked to create account instances.

Figure 5.7 illustrates the class program structure in more detail. Notice that the structure has two distinct segments: factory definition and instance definition. Each segment can contain its own data division and one or more method definitions. The data division in the instance segment is generally where we define the attributes.

As shown in Figure 5.7, the IDENTIFICATION, ENVIRONMENT, and DATA DIVISION headers are optional. In future programs, we will omit these headers to reduce clutter and improve readability.

Also, notice that the figure indicates *scope* for the various data divisions. The scope of a data item refers to the parts of the class program that can access that item. For example, the factory DATA DIVISION indicates its scope is all factory and instance methods. This means a data item defined in this DATA DIVISION will be accessible to all factory and instance methods. However, a data item defined in the Data Division of an instance method has scope limited to that method. The location of a data item in the class program determines its scope.

```
IDENTIFICATION DIVISION. <-----------------------------------(Division header is optional)
CLASS-ID.        classname
            DATA IS PRIVATE
            INHERITS FROM parentclassname. <------------------------(name of parent class)
ENVIRONMENT DIVISION.  <---------------------------------(Division header is optional)
INPUT-OUTPUT SECTION.
FILE-CONTROL.
REPOSITORY.
      Classname IS CLASS "classfilename".<----------------------(List all classes to be accessed)
DATA DIVISION. <---------(Division header optional; Scope: All Factory & Instance Methods
```

```
FACTORY.  <---------------------------------------------------(Begin Factory Definition)
DATA DIVISION. <-----------------(Division header is optional; Scope: All Factory Methods)

    METHOD-ID. methodname.<---------------------------------(Factory method header)
    DATA DIVISION.        <-----------------(Division header is optional; Scope: This Method)
    PROCEDURE DIVISION USING dataname1, dataname2, ...  RETURNING dataname.
        ...
        EXIT METHOD
    END METHOD methodname. <-------------(scope terminator for this method definition)
                (.......Multiple Factory Methods May Exist)




    END FACTORY. <--------------------------------------------(End factory Method definitions)
```

```
OBJECT. <---------------------------------------------------(Begin Instance definitions)
DATA DIVISION.<---------------------(Division header is optional; Scope: Instance Methods)
                (usually this is where instance attributes are defined)

    METHOD-ID. methodname.<---------------------------------(Instance method header)
    DATA DIVISION.        <-----------------(Division header is optional; Scope: This Method)
    PROCEDURE DIVISION USING dataname1, dataname2, ...  RETURNING dataname.
        ...
        EXIT METHOD
    END METHOD methodname. <-------------(scope terminator for this method definition)
                (.......Multiple Instance Methods May Exist)


END OBJECT. <---------------------------------------------(End of Instance Definition code)
```

```
END CLASS classname.  <---------------------------------------------(end of Class program)
```

Figure 5.7 Class Program Structure

Creating an Instance

The previous Account example gave you a first look at a class program and demonstrated how to invoke a method. In this section, we will expand this example by adding a factory method to create a new account instance (**OpenNewAccount),** and we will add code to the driver program to invoke **OpenNewAccount.**

We will also add a private instance method (**PopulateAccount**) that will be invoked by **OpenNewAccount** to store values into the account attributes *account-number* and *current-balance*. **PopulateAccount** is called a *private method* because it will be invoked only by the class <u>Account</u>. It is not intended to be invoked by outside classes. This is in contrast to the *public methods* that are available to other classes.

Figure 5.8 is our expanded <u>Account</u> class program with the new factory method **OpenNewAccount** defined at lines 6 through 20, and the new private instance method **PopulateAccount**, coded in lines 29 through 40. Figure 5.9 is the revised driver program with code added (boldface) to invoke **OpenNewAccount**. Incidentally, these are complete, working programs. You are encouraged to execute and experiment with them.[1]

LINE	Object COBOL Code

```
 1  CLASS-ID.    Account.

 2  REPOSITORY.
 3      Account IS CLASS "CH5-ACCT".

 4   * begin Factory Definition -------------------------------------
 5  FACTORY.
 6  METHOD-ID.   "OpenNewAccount".
 7  LINKAGE SECTION.
 8  01   account-number-ls        PIC 9(5).
 9  01   customer-ss-no-ls        PIC 9(9).
10  01   current-balance-ls       PIC S9(5)V99.
11  01   anAccount                USAGE IS OBJECT REFERENCE.
12      PROCEDURE DIVISION USING account-number-ls, customer-ss-no-ls
13                               current-balance-ls
14              RETURNING anAccount.
15      INVOKE Base "New" Returning anAccount
16      INVOKE anAccount      "PopulateAccount"
17         USING account-number-ls, customer-ss-no-ls,
18              current-balance-ls
19      EXIT METHOD.
20  END METHOD.  "OpenNewAccount".
21  END FACTORY.

22   * begin instance definition --------------------------------
23  OBJECT.
24  WORKING-STORAGE SECTION.
25   * following are Account attributes ------------------------
26  01   account-number-ws    PIC 9(5).
27  01   customer-ss-no-ws    PIC 9(9).
28  01   current-balance-ws   PIC S9(5)V99.

29  METHOD-ID.   "PopulateAccount".
30  LINKAGE SECTION.
31  01   account-number-ls    PIC 9(5).
32  01   customer-ss-no-ls    PIC 9(9).
33  01   current-balance-ls   PIC S9(5)V99.
34  PROCEDURE DIVISION USING account-number-ls, customer-ss-no-ls
35                          current-balance-ls.
36      MOVE account-number-ls  TO account-number-ws
```

---

[1]See "A Note about Object COBOL Standards" at the end of the chapter.

```
37        MOVE current-balance-ls TO current-balance-ws
38        MOVE customer-ss-no-ls  TO customer-ss-no-ws
39        EXIT METHOD.
40 END METHOD.  "PopulateAccount".

41 METHOD-ID.  "TellCurrentBalance".
42 LINKAGE SECTION.
43 01 current-balance-ls         PIC S9(5)V99.
44 PROCEDURE DIVISION RETURNING current-balance-ls.
45        MOVE current-balance-ws to current-balance-ls
46        EXIT METHOD.
47 END METHOD.  "TellCurrentBalance".

48 END OBJECT.

49 END CLASS Account.
```

Figure 5.8 Expanded ACCOUNT Class Program

LINE   Object COBOL Code

```
1    PROGRAM-ID.         CH5-PRG1.
2    REPOSITORY.
3        Account IS CLASS "CH5-ACCT".
4    WORKING-STORAGE SECTION.

5    01 anAccount        USAGE IS OBJECT REFERENCE.
6    01  account-number-ws   PIC 9(5).
7    01  customer-ss-no-ws   pic 9(9).
8    01 current-balance-ws   PIC S9(5)V99.

9    PROCEDURE DIVISION.
10       MOVE 1          TO account-number-ws
11       MOVE 123456789 TO customer-ss-no-ws
12       MOVE 678.90     TO current-balance-ws
13       INVOKE Account "OpenNewAccount" USING account-number-ws,
14           customer-ss-no-ws, current-balance-ws
15           RETURNING anAccount
16       INVOKE anAccount "TellCurrentBalance"
17           RETURNING current-balance-ws
18       DISPLAY "The Current Balance is:",current-balance-ws
19       STOP RUN.
```

Figure 5.9 Driver to INVOKE OpenNewAccount

Figure 5.10 shows the object interaction diagram (OID) for the execution of **OpenNewAccount**. This OID shows the driver program, our revised Account class program, and a new class named Base. In this example, we use the **New** method in Base to create the new instance of Account. Base is an Object COBOL library class program that provides several useful methods such as **New**, which is used to create an instance.

Step 1 in the OID indicates that the driver program invokes the factory method **OpenNewAccount** passing the account number, social security number, and current balance. Account, in step 2, invokes **New** in Base, which returns anAccount that contains a pointer to the instance of account that was just created. Next, at step 3, still in **OpenNewAccount,** the (private) instance method **PopulateAccount** is invoked which stores the values for account number, social security number, and current balance.

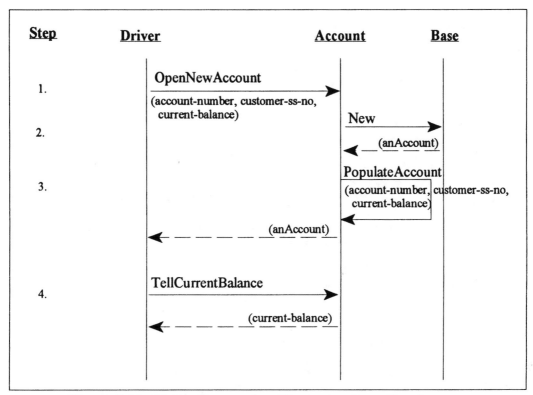

Figure 5.10 Object Interaction Diagram—OpenNewAccount

Notice that the invocation of **PopulateAccount** is an example of a factory method **(OpenNewAccount)** invoking an instance method. At the end of **OpenNewAccount**, the instance pointer anAccount is returned to driver. Then, at step 4, driver invokes **TellCurrentBalance**, which returns the parameter current-balance.

Creating Multiple Instances

Figure 5.11 is the now familiar driver program with code added to create two instances of Account. In this example, we are opening two accounts, account number 1 and number 2. At lines 5 and 6 we have defined two separate instance pointers named anAccount1 and anAccount2.

LINE	Object COBOL Code

```
1     PROGRAM-ID. CH5-PRG2.

2     REPOSITORY.
3         Account IS CLASS "CH5-ACCT".

4     WORKING-STORAGE SECTION.
5     01  anAccount1     USAGE IS OBJECT REFERENCE.
6     01  anAccount2     USAGE IS OBJECT REFERENCE
7     01  account-number-ws   PIC 9(5).
8     01  customer-ss-no-ws   PIC 9(9).
9     01  current-balance-ws  PIC S9(5)V99.

10    PROCEDURE DIVISION.

11 * create two instances of Account
12        MOVE 1          TO account-number-ws
13        MOVE 123456789 TO customer-ss-no-ws
14        MOVE 678.90     TO current-balance-ws
15    * invoke the factory method OpenNewAccount in the Account class
16        INVOKE Account "OpenNewAccount"
17            USING account-number-ws, customer-ss-no-ws
18                  current-balance-ws
19            RETURNING anAccount1
20        MOVE 2          TO account-number-ws
21        MOVE 987654321 TO customer-ss-no-ws
22        MOVE 234.45     TO current-balance-ws
23        INVOKE Account "OpenNewAccount"
24            USING account-number-ws, customer-ss-no-ws
25            RETURNING anAccount2
26 * invoke the instance method TellCurrentBalance to
27 * retrieve the account balances from the instances
28        INVOKE anAccount1 "TellCurrentBalance"
29            RETURNING current-balance-ws
30        DISPLAY "The Balance of Account 1 is:",
31           current-balance-ws
32        INVOKE anAccount2 "TellCurrentBalance"
33            RETURNING current-balance-ws
34        DISPLAY "The Balance of Account 2 is:",
35           current-balance-ws

36        STOP RUN.
```

Figure 5.11   Driver Program to Create Multiple Account Instances

This version of driver is accessing the methods **OpenNewAccount** and **TellCurrentBalance** in the class program for Account. However, we have not changed the class program Account! The first invoke statement at line 16 creates the first account and stores its location in anAccount1. Similarly, the second invoke at line 23 creates the second account and stores its location in anAccount2. At line 28 we invoke the **TellCurrent Balance** method for the first account and at line 32 for the second. Notice that these invoke statements appear to be the same except for the account instance pointers (see Figure 5.12).

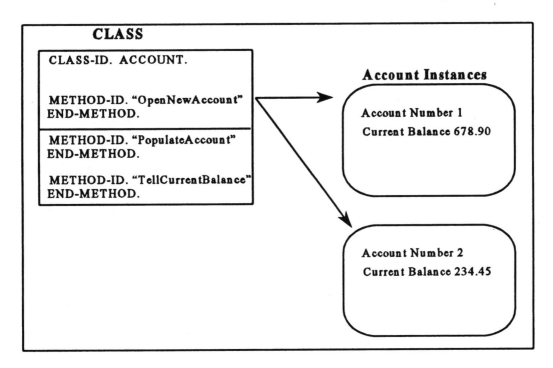

Figure 5.12 Multiple Instances of ACCOUNT

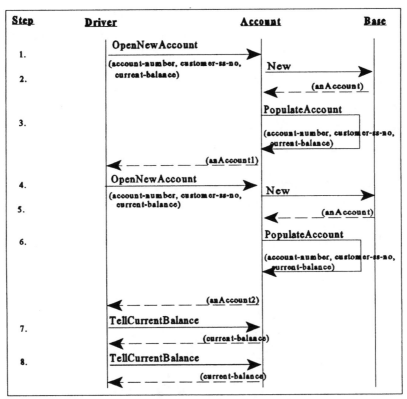

Figure 5.13   Object Interaction Diagram—
Multiple Instances

Figure 5.13 shows the OID for creating and accessing the two instances. Steps 1 through 6 create the instances, and steps 7 and 8 retrieve their current balances.

Layered Systems Development

Many traditional information processing programs have three main components: a user interface that interacts with the user; a data management segment that deals with data storage and retrieval; and the main information processing section, sometimes called the problem domain, that contains the main business processing logic and computation code. Here we call these three components "layers." We have then, a *user interface layer*, a *problem domain layer*, and a *data management layer*.

The exact form of these layers is unimportant. For example, the user interface can be text-based or GUI, and the data management section can use sequential files or relational databases. The physical implementation is unimportant. What is important is that each layer be as independent as possible from the other layers. Some even advocate that each layer be a separate program that uses CALL statements to interface with the other layers.

Making a distinct separation between these layers has important advantages. To illustrate, if all three of these components are in a single program, a change to one layer requires that the entire program be recompiled and tested, even though the change is related to only one part. If, for example, we have database-specific code embedded in an application program and we change database systems, this code will have to be changed. This change will force us to search the entire program for the database-related code, make the necessary changes, and then recompile and test the revised program. Similarly, if we have screen-specific code in a program and we change the interface, say from text-based to GUI, the code related to the interface will have to be located and updated, and again, the entire program will have to be recompiled and tested. Often, the screen-specific and database-specific code is not concentrated in one part of a program. Instead, it is frequently scattered throughout the program, further complicating our task of program modification.

Sectioning systems into user interface, problem domain, and data management layers reduces the difficulties whenever a change is required. Changes in one component generally will not require changes in other components. We want each component to be as independent as possible. In structured methodology, this idea is called coupling; we want very loose coupling.

Similar concepts have been presented by other authors; for a summary of other layered approaches, see Table 5.1. Overall, the layers presented here are similar; only the names are slightly different.

Table 5.1   Object Layers
Corresponding Layers as Identified by Other Authors

Our layers	OMG Object Model	Coad and Yourdon	Goldberg and Rubin
1. User interface	Common facilities	Human interaction	Presentation & interaction
2. Problem domain	Application objects	Problem domain	Application logic
3. Data management	Object services	Data management	Database management

We can develop layered systems using traditional (non-OO) techniques by simply writing separate programs to deal with each layer and then use CALL statements to provide communication between the layers. Figure 5.14 illustrates this approach.

Object-oriented techniques, however, simplify the development of layered systems because we can design classes for each layer and then use INVOKE statements to communicate between the classes. The OO paradigm facilitates this communication. For example, we can design classes for the user interface, additional classes to do the actual application processing, and classes for the data management function. This approach is depicted in Figure 5.15. This figure also shows the chapter numbers associated with each layer.

Figure 5.14 Traditional Program Layers

In this chapter, we have focused on the middle problem domain layer. We have developed the Account class to do processing for accounts. In subsequent chapters we continue the development of the credit union system using the layered approach. Chapter 6 will continue the development of the problem domain layer by designing CheckingAccount, LoanAccount, and SavingsAccount classes. Chapter 7 will deal with the design and development of classes in the data management layer. In that chapter, we will provide for persistent instances by storing account and customer information in indexed files. The implementation of this data management layer will, however, be totally independent from the problem domain layer. The problem domain classes will invoke methods in the

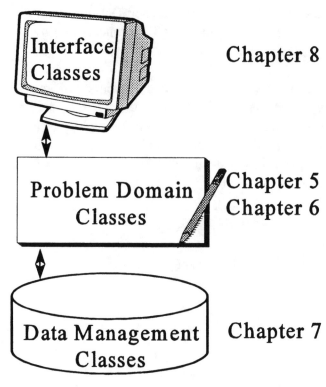

Interface Classes   Chapter 8

Problem Domain Classes   Chapter 5
                                     Chapter 6

Data Management Classes   Chapter 7

Figure 5.15 Class Layers

data management classes to store and retrieve account and customer information. The interfaces of these data management methods will intentionally be kept very simple and general, hiding the data storage implementation details from the problem domain classes.

Chapter 8 will complete the credit union system with the addition of screen classes representing the user interface layer. There, we will design screens for both customer and account processing. These screens will implement the same functions, such as open an account, that are seen in previous chapters. However, these functions will be accomplished through the screen interface layer communicating with the problem domain classes. Again, the interfaces to the problem domain classes and the data management classes will not change, even though we will add new classes to create the interface layer.

Summary

This chapter has introduced you to the fundamentals of Object COBOL. You learned how to write a simple class program and to write a driver program to invoke methods. You saw that class programs can contain both factory methods and instance methods. This was illustrated in the Account class program. Factory methods provide class services such as the creation of instances. In contrast, instance methods deal with individual instances. In this chapter, we invoked the factory method, **OpenNewAccount**, and the instance methods, **PopulateAccount** and **TellCurrentBalance**. You saw that we can have private methods that are available only to the class and public methods that are accessible to other classes.

Also in this chapter we introduced you to object interaction diagrams and illustrated their application to several examples. These diagrams are used to map the interactions between objects or, as in this chapter, between a procedural program and a class program.

This chapter introduced you to the structure of class programs written in Object COBOL. The overall class syntax was presented, and the scope of data items was briefly described.

The concept of layered systems design was presented. Systems can be segmented into three layers: user interface, problem domain, and data management. The object-oriented paradigm facilitates layered development.

In the next chapter, we explore the idea of superclasses, subclasses and inheritance by writing a class program for the subclasses of <u>Account</u>. We will illustrate how to invoke inherited methods in the chapter by extending the ideas presented here. Chapter 6 continues the development of the problem domain classes for the credit union system.

A Note About Object COBOL Standards

At this time, there is no agreed upon standard for Object COBOL. ANSI has released preliminary reports outlining the standards, but these have not yet been finalized. Because many vendors, such as Micro Focus and IBM, are trying to provide Object COBOL products as early as possible, some of the features of compilers may not comply with early releases of the Object COBOL standard. Such is the case with the Micro Focus Personal COBOL for Windows system which is used to develop the system presented in this book.

Earlier in this chapter, a simple class program and a class template were presented (Figures 5.2 and 5.7, respectively). These figures follow the standards determined by ANSI. However, the final programs presented at the end of this chapter follow the guidelines established by Micro Focus. Although the changes are minor, you should be aware of them. Two differences need to be noted at this time:

1. The ANSI standard specifies the use of the word REPOSITORY in the ENVIRONMENT DIVISION. Micro Focus, on the other hand, uses CLASS-CONTROL.

2. The ANSI standard specifies the use of the word FACTORY to indicate the beginning of factory attributes and methods. Micro Focus uses CLASS-OBJECT.

Therefore, you will see some slight differences between the programs presented in the text of this chapter and the programs at the end of the chapter. Throughout the remainder of the book, we will follow the syntax of the Micro Focus compiler so that all programs can be compiled and executed using Personal COBOL. We will note the differences between Micro Focus and ANSI standards where necessary.

KEY TERMS

Class methods

Class program

Data management layer

Driver program

Factory methods

Instance methods

Object interaction diagram

Private method

Problem domain layer

Public method

Scope

User interface layer

REVIEW QUESTIONS

1. What COBOL verb is used to send a message between objects?

2. Why is it necessary to have both instance and factory methods?

3. What is the scope of factory data and methods? What is the scope of instance data and methods?

4. What classes can invoke public methods? What classes can invoke private methods?

5. Can methods from one class invoke methods in another class? For example, can a factory method in class A invoke an instance method in class B?

6. What are the "layers" of an information system?

EXERCISES

1. The program in Figure 5.11 is used to create two instances of account. The first Account is called anAccount1, and the second is called anAccount2. Modify the program in Figure 5.11 to use the same object reference (for example, anAccount1) for both instances. What is displayed when you run the driver program? Why did this occur?

2. Construct a one-dimensional table of object references to hold up to ten references. Create the instances, put information in the instances, and then display the information to the screen.

3. Create an OID that shows the interaction between a PERSON and an AUTOMOBILE for the operation of driving a car. What methods were used to drive (by the PERSON) and to be driven (by the AUTOMOBILE)?

4. Take any recent procedural COBOL program you have written. How could the program be "restructured" as a class program? Are you comfortable with restructuring the program at this time?

BIBLIOGRAPHY

Arranga, E., and Coyle, F. Object-Oriented COBOL. SIGS Publications, 1996.

Booch, G. Object-Oriented Design with Applications. Benjamin-Cummings, 1991.

Brown, D. An Introduction to Object-Oriented Analysis. John Wiley & Sons, 1997.

Chapin, N. Standard Object-Oriented COBOL. John Wiley & Sons, 1997.

Coad, P., and Yourdon, E. Object-Oriented Analysis. Yourdon Press, Prentice-Hall, 1991.

Goldberg, A., and Rubin, K. Succeeding with Objects: Decision Frameworks for Project Management. Addison-Wesley, 1995.

Jacobson, I., et al. Object-Oriented Software Engineering: A Use Case Driven Approach. Addison-Wesley, 1992.

Price, W. Elements on Object-Oriented COBOL. Object-Z Publishing, 1997.

Rumbaugh, J., et al. Object-Oriented Modeling and Design. Prentice-Hall, 1991.

CLASS DESCRIPTIONS

Class Name: Account

Attributes: account-number   PIC 9(5)
                 customer-ss-no   PIC 9(9)
                 current-balance   PIC S9(5)V99

Factory Method:
1. OpenNewAccount USING account-number, customer-ss-no,
                current-balance
                RETURNING anAccount

Instance Methods:
1. <Private> PopulateAccount USING account-number,
    customer-ss-no, current-balance
2. TellCurrentBalance RETURNING current-balance

PROGRAM LISTINGS

Account Class Program

```
*   CH5-ACCT is a class program for Account
*      Factory Methods:      OpenNewAccount (Invokes New from BASE)
*      Instance methods:     PopulateAccount, TellCurrentBalance,
*                            ChangeCurrentBalance
*      Attributes: account-number, customer-ss-no, current-balance
*-----------------------------------------------------------
```

```
1     CLASS-ID. CH5-ACCT
2             data is private
3             inherits from Base.
4     OBJECT SECTION.
5     CLASS-CONTROL.
6         Base         is class "Base"
7         Account      is class "CH5-ACCT".
8
9     CLASS-OBJECT.
10    OBJECT-STORAGE SECTION.
11    *------ Factory Method -------------------------------------
12    METHOD-ID. "OpenNewAccount".
13    LINKAGE SECTION.
14    01   account-number-ls        PIC 9(5).
15    01   customer-ss-no-ls        PIC 9(9).
16    01   current-balance-ls       PIC S9(5)V99.
17    01   anAccount                Usage is Object Reference.
18
19    PROCEDURE DIVISION    USING account-number-ls, customer-ss-no-ls
20                                    current-balance-ls
21                              RETURNING anAccount.
22        INVOKE Self "New" RETURNING anAccount
23        INVOKE anAccount      "PopulateAccount"
24                          USING account-number-ls, customer-ss-no-ls
25                                    current-balance-ls
26        END-INVOKE
27        EXIT METHOD.
28    END METHOD "OpenNewAccount".
29    END CLASS-OBJECT.
30    *------Instance Methods ------------------------------------
31    OBJECT.
32    OBJECT-STORAGE SECTION.
33    01   account-info-os.
34         05   account-number-os        PIC 9(5).
35         05   customer-ss-no-os         PIC 9(9).
36         05   current-balance-os        PIC S9(5)V99.
37    *-----------------------------------------------------------
38    METHOD-ID. "PopulateAccount".
39    LINKAGE SECTION.
40    01   account-number-ls        PIC 9(5).
41    01   customer-ss-no-ls        PIC 9(9).
42    01   current-balance-ls       PIC S9(5)V99.
43
44    PROCEDURE DIVISION USING account-number-ls, customer-ss-no-ls
45                                    current-balance-ls.
46        MOVE account-number-ls  TO account-number-os
47        MOVE customer-ss-no-ls  TO customer-ss-no-os
48        MOVE current-balance-ls TO current-balance-os
49        EXIT METHOD.
```

```
50        END METHOD "PopulateAccount".
51        *------------------------------------------------------------
52        METHOD-ID. "TellCurrentBalance".
53        LINKAGE SECTION.
54        01  current-balance-ls  PIC S9(5)V99.
55
56        PROCEDURE DIVISION  RETURNING current-balance-ls.
57            MOVE current-balance-os TO current-balance-ls
58            EXIT METHOD.
59        END METHOD "TellCurrentBalance".
60        END OBJECT.
61        END CLASS CH5-ACCT
62
63        *------------------------------------------------------------
```

Driver Program 1

```
*   CH5-PRG1 is a procedural COBOL program used to illustrate
*    the invocation of both factory & instance methods in Account
*------------------------------------------------------------
```

```
1    PROGRAM-ID. CH5-PRG1.
2    *------------------------------------------------------------
3    CLASS-CONTROL.
4        Account     is class "CH5-ACCT".
5
6    WORKING-STORAGE SECTION.
7    01  anAccount        Usage is Object Reference.
8
9    *  Account Attributes
10   01  account-number-ws         PIC 9(5).
11   01  customer-ss-no-ws         PIC 9(9).
12   01  current-balance-ws        PIC S9(5)V99.
13
14   PROCEDURE DIVISION.
15       MOVE 1         TO  account-number-ws
16       MOVE 123456789 TO  customer-ss-no-ws
17       MOVE 678.90    TO  current-balance-ws
18       INVOKE Account "OpenNewAccount"
19           USING     account-number-ws, customer-ss-no-ws
20                     current-balance-ws
21           RETURNING anAccount
22       END-INVOKE
23
24       INVOKE anAccount "TellCurrentBalance"
25           returning current-balance-ws
26       END-INVOKE
27       DISPLAY "The Current Balance of account 1 is: ",
28           current-balance-ws
29       STOP RUN.
30   *------------------------------------------------------------
```

Driver Program 2

```
     *   CH5-PRG2 is a procedural COBOL program used to illustrate
     *     the creation of multiple instances of Account
     *------------------------------------------------------------
1        PROGRAM-ID. CH5-PRG2.
2    *------------------------------------------------------------
3        CLASS-CONTROL.
4            Account    is class "CH5-ACCT".
5
6        WORKING-STORAGE SECTION.
7        01   anAccount1      Usage is Object Reference.
8        01   anAccount2      Usage is Object Reference.
9    *  Account Attributes
10       01    account-number-ws         PIC 9(5).
11       01    customer-ss-no-ws         PIC 9(9).
12       01    current-balance-ws        PIC S9(5)V99.
13
14       PROCEDURE DIVISION.
15           MOVE 1         TO   account-number-ws
16           MOVE 123456789 TO   customer-ss-no-ws
17           MOVE 678.90    TO   current-balance-ws
18           INVOKE Account "OpenNewAccount"
19               USING      account-number-ws, customer-ss-no-ws
20                          current-balance-ws
21               RETURNING anAccount1
22           END-INVOKE
23
24           MOVE 2         TO   account-number-ws
25           MOVE 987654321 TO   customer-ss-no-ws
26           MOVE 234.45    TO   current-balance-ws
27           INVOKE Account "OpenNewAccount"
28               USING      account-number-ws, customer-ss-no-ws
29                          current-balance-ws
30               RETURNING anAccount2
31           END-INVOKE
32
33           INVOKE anAccount1 "TellCurrentBalance"
34               returning current-balance-ws
35           END-INVOKE
36           DISPLAY "The Current Balance of account 1 is: ",
37               current-balance-ws
38
39           INVOKE anAccount2 "TellCurrentBalance"
40               returning current-balance-ws
41           END-INVOKE
42           DISPLAY "The Current Balance of account 2 is: ",
43               current-balance-ws
44
45           STOP RUN.
46   *------------------------------------------------------------
```

CHAPTER 6:

Working with Superclasses and Subclasses

Chapter 5 introduced the idea of object layers and began the development of the problem domain classes. This chapter continues the development of problem domain classes as shown in Figure 6.1.

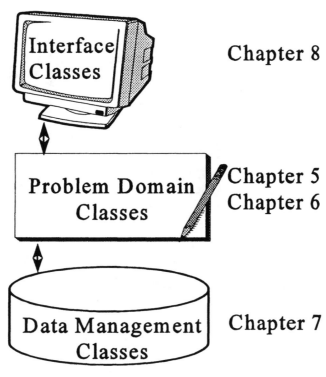

Figure 6.1 Class Layers

One benefit of the object-oriented paradigm is reuse.   OO reuse has two forms: the reuse of class programs, and the inheritance of methods by subclasses. Some argue that reuse through inheritance is actually the more important of the two.

This chapter introduces you to inheritance and its benefits and application. We develop three subclasses of Account, then invoke both inherited and noninherited methods in these subclasses.

In Chapter 2, you saw that the credit union system had the superclass Account, with subclasses CheckingAccount, SavingsAccount, and LoanAccount. Figure 6.2 depicts these classes where you can see the inherited and noninherited methods in the subclasses. In this chapter, we develop class

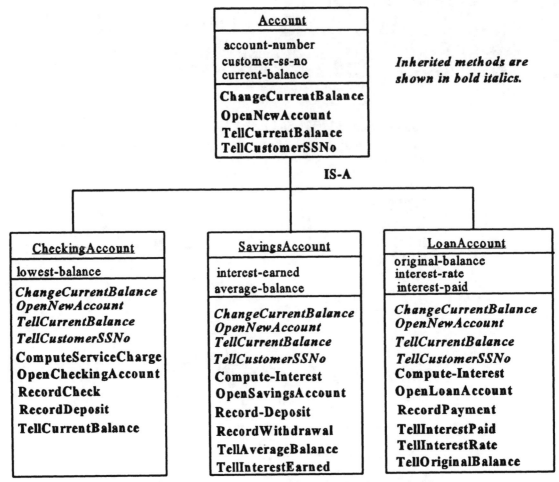

Figure 6.2   Subclasses with Inherited Methods

programs for all three subclasses. These programs contain all of the methods shown in the figure. We will create instances for all three types of accounts—checking, loan, and savings—and then invoke the various methods in these classes.

We will describe, in some detail, the creation of an instance, especially the composite instance whenever we have a subclass and superclass together. The chapter concludes with a discussion of persistent instances and their destruction when they are no longer needed.

After studying this chapter, you should understand how to work with superclasses and subclasses in the Is-a relationship. You will see how to design and write class programs representing superclasses and subclasses. Then you will learn how to invoke both inherited and noninherited methods.

A Word About Inherited Attributes

Chapter 2 discussed inheritance in the Is-a relationship. You will recall that *subclasses* in the Is-a relationship inherit attributes, methods, and relationships from their superclass. In reality, the current ANSI 9X COBOL standard does not support the physical inheritance of attributes. This is because allowing attributes to be inherited violates the principle of encapsulation: **data in an object are hidden from other objects.** The only way to access these encapsulated data is through a method. This is not a significant restriction because we will have methods to access these attributes.

In keeping with this idea, we have included methods in Account to provide *account-number, customer-ss-no,* and *current-balance* values, therefore we will simply invoke the appropriate method (inherited!) whenever a subclass needs one of these values. Although some vendors currently support *inherited attributes,* we will not illustrate this type of inheritance here. We will, however, employ *inherited methods* in the examples in this chapter as shown in Figure 6.2.

The Account Class Program

The Account class used in this chapter is a copy of the Account class introduced in Chapter 5 (CH5-ACCT), with two new instance methods added: **ChangeCurrentBalance** and **TellCustomerSSNo**. As the name suggests, the first method changes an account's balance. It will be invoked when a check or deposit is posted to a checking account or when a payment is made to a loan account. The second method returns a customer's social security number. We now have methods to return values for all three attributes: *account-number, customer-ss-no,* and *current-balance.* Remember that all of these methods are inherited by the subclasses; therefore, it appears as if the methods are actually in the subclasses. The code for this expanded class program is listed at the end of the chapter and is named "CH6-ACCT."

Incidentally, using the Account class program from Chapter 5 here illustrates the reuse of a class program. We have taken an existing class program, CH5-ACCT, and simply added two methods to make CH6-ACCT. The addition of these new methods does not affect the other methods in Account or change their public interface in any way. If we wished, we could use this revised class program in Chapter 5, **without changing any code.** In fact, we will use this class program in subsequent chapters as we add user interface and data management classes to the example. We will not need to modify this class, although we will significantly expand the system.

The CheckingAccount Class Program

Beyond the four methods inherited from its superclass Account, the subclass CheckingAccount has five public methods and one private method defined in the class program named "CH6-CHEK." We will describe each method individually below. Object interaction diagrams (OIDs) are included for

OpenCheckingAccount and **RecordCheck** to illustrate the message flow that occurs as these methods are invoked.

Public methods are those that are used by other classes, whereas *private methods* are intended for use only by the class owning the method. In the Account class, **PopulateAccount** is a private method: it is not designed to be used by classes other than Account. Each of the subclasses has a similar method: **PopulateCheckingAccount,   PopulateLoanAccount,** and **PopulateSavingsAccount**. These private instance methods are designed simply to store values into the attributes for each instance as it is created.

1. **ComputeServiceCharge**. This is an instance method designed to compute the service charge for a checking account. The method logic charges $5.00 if the *lowest balance* for the account is less than $100, otherwise the service charge is zero.

2. **OpenCheckingAccount**. Recall that Account has a factory method named **OpenNewAccount** whose purpose is to create an instance of Account when an account is opened. Similarly, each of the three Account subclasses in this chapter has a factory method to create an instance. For example, CheckingAccount has **OpenCheckingAccount**, LoanAccount has **OpenLoanAccount**, and SavingsAccount has **OpenSavingsAccount**. Each of these factory methods is designed to create instances of the particular type of account (checking, loan, or savings) being opened. Because these open account methods are very similar, we will discuss the **OpenCheckingAccount** method in some detail, with less discussion of the others.

    When **OpenCheckingAccount** is invoked, only one instance is created. However, this instance combines both Account and CheckingAccount and contains the attributes and methods for both. A single-instance pointer is used to reach the instance.

    Figure 6.3 is an OID that maps the execution of **OpenCheckingAccount**. This method first invokes the inherited method **OpenNewAccount** (step 2), which in turn invokes **New** in the Base class (step 3). **New** returns the instance pointer anAccount to Account. Account then invokes its private instance method **PopulateAccount** (step 4), which stores the values for the Account attributes: *account-number*, *customer-ss-no*, and *current-balance*. **OpenNewAccount** then returns the instance pointer anAccount to **OpenCheckingAccount**, which then invokes **PopulateCheckingAccount** (step 5), similar to **PopulateAccount**, to store the value of the attribute *lowest-balance* for CheckingAccount

3. **RecordCheck**. This instance method was designed to post a check to a checking account. The OID in Figure 6.4 details the execution of **RecordCheck**. First, **RecordCheck** invokes the inherited method **TellCurrentBalance** (step 2) to obtain the account's present balance. Then, the amount of the check is subtracted from this balance, and the inherited method **ChangeCurrentBalance** is invoked (step 3) to update the account balance. **RecordCheck** compares the current balance with the lowest balance for the account and updates the lowest balance if the current balance after the check is posted is less than the lowest balance.

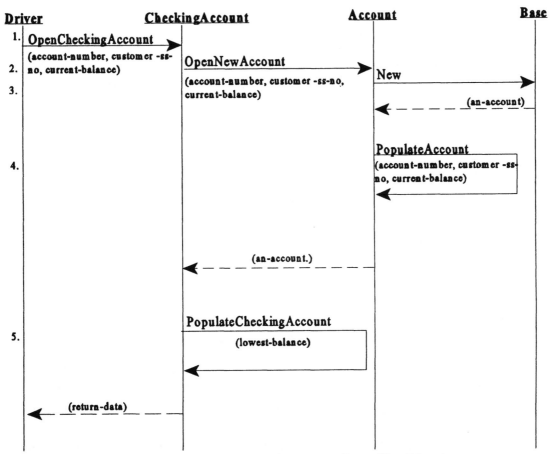

Figure 6.3 Object Interaction Diagram—OpenCheckingAccount

4. **RecordDeposit** is identical to **RecordCheck** except the amount of the deposit is added to the account's balance and the lowest balance attribute is not changed.

5. **TellLowestBalance** is an instance method invoked to return the account's lowest balance.

THE LOANACCOUNT CLASS PROGRAM

The LoanAccount subclass also inherits the four methods from Account: **ChangeCurrentBalance, OpenNewAccount, TellCurrentBalance,** and **TellCustomerSSNo.** LoanAccount has six noninherited public methods: **ComputeInterest, OpenLoanAcccount, RecordPayment, TellInterest Paid, TellInterestRate,** and **TellOriginalBalance.** LoanAccount also has the private method, **PopulateLoanAccount.** LoanAccount has three attributes: *original-balance, interest-rate,* and *interest-paid.* Each public method will be described individually below. The class program for LoanAccount is named "CH6-LOAN" and is listed at the end of the chapter.

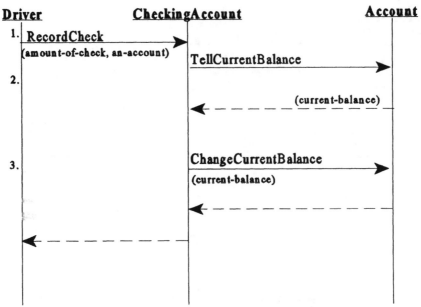

Figure 6.4 Object Interaction Diagram—RecordCheck

1. **ComputeInterest**, an instance method, is used to compute the interest each month for the loan based on the outstanding balance, and then return the interest value to the invoking program.

   First, the inherited method **TellCurrentBalance** is invoked to obtain the loan's current balance. The COMPUTE statement then multiplies the loan account's current balance by its interest rate to compute the *interest-this-month*. Incidentally, **ComputeInterest** is an example of a polymorphic method. Both SavingsAccount and LoanAccount have methods named **ComputeInterest**. However, their logic is different. **ComputeInterest** for a savings account multiplies the interest rate, which the invoking program must supply, by the *average-balance* of the savings account. **ComputeInterest** for LoanAccount multiplies the account's *current-balance* by the *interest-rate* for that loan.

2. **OpenLoanAccount**, similar to the other open account methods, is a factory method that creates an instance of LoanAccount and populates the three loan attributes.

3. **RecordPayment**, as the name suggests, is an instance method that posts a payment to LoanAccount. The OID is shown in Figure 6.5. First, **ComputeInterest** (see the description above) is invoked to calculate this month's interest amount (step 2). Then the new loan balance is computed by subtracting the payment amount less this month's interest. Then the inherited method, **ChangeCurrentBalance**, is invoked (step 4) to store the updated current balance for the loan account. Finally, the interest paid this month is added to the interest-paid attribute.

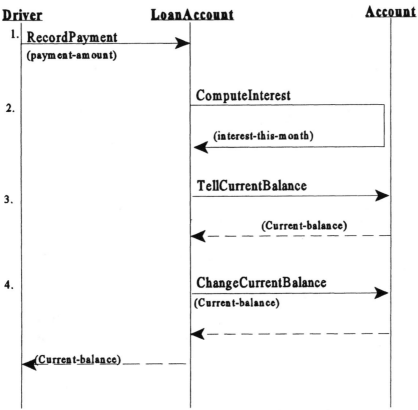

**Figure 6.5 Object Interaction Diagram—
RecordPayment for LoanAccount**

4. **TellInterestPaid** is an instance method that returns the interest paid value to the invoking program.

5. **TellInterestRate** is an instance method that returns the loan's interest rate value to the invoking program.

6. **TellOriginalBalance** is an instance method that returns the loan's original balance to the invoking program.

THE SAVINGSACCOUNT CLASS PROGRAM

The SavingsAccount class program, named "CH6-SVGS," is shown at the end of the chapter. Like the previous two subclasses, SavingsAccount inherits the four methods from Account. This class also has the familiar factory method **OpenSavingsAccount**, five public instance methods, and the private instance method **PopulateSavingsAccount**. These public methods are discussed below. SavingsAccount has two attributes: *interest-earned* and *average-balance*.

1. **ComputeInterest** is an instance method used to compute the interest each month for the savings account. As previously indicated, **ComputeInterest** is polymorphic because both <u>SavingsAccount</u> and <u>LoanAccount</u> have methods named **ComputeInterest**.

2. **OpenSavingsAccount**, similar to the other open account methods, is a factory method that creates an instance of <u>SavingsAccount</u> and populates its attributes.

3. **RecordDeposit**, as the name suggests, is an instance method that posts a deposit to the savings account. **TellCurrentBalance** is invoked to obtain the account's current. Then the amount of the deposit is added to the current balance and **ChangeCurrentBalance** is invoked to update the current balance.

4. **RecordWithdrawal** is identical to **RecordDeposit**, but the amount of the withdrawal is subtracted from the current balance of the account.

5. **TellInterestEarned** is an instance method that returns the interest earned value to the invoking program.

6. **TellAverageBalance** is an instance method that returns the account's average balance to the invoking program. Note that we have not included the computation of the average balance value here.

A Program to INVOKE the Class Methods

The driver program, named "CH6-PRG1," which invokes the various methods in the <u>Account</u> superclass and the subclasses <u>CheckingAccount</u>, <u>LoanAccount</u>, and <u>SavingsAccount</u> is listed at the end of the chapter.

The execution of the driver program is straightforward. It initially opens a new checking account, a new loan account, and a new savings account by invoking the open account factory methods in each of the three subclasses. The INVOKE statements pass the initial attribute values to the methods, which in turn populate the respective attributes in these account instances. Next, the driver program retrieves and displays the account balances.

Then the driver invokes the various methods in <u>CheckingAccount</u>, <u>LoanAccount</u>, and <u>SavingsAccount</u>. The driver includes display statements to show the values returned from the various methods. As mentioned in the previous chapter, the use of driver and class programs illustrates a *client-server* environment. The client (driver) uses the server (classes) to achieve its goals. The actions of the server are hidden from the client. The client only needs to know what command (INVOKE statement) to send to get action. We encourage you to load and execute the driver and class programs presented here. Given the classes we have produced here, you can perform a variety of functions from a driver program.

INSTANCE CREATION FOR SUBCLASSES

Whenever we create an instance of a class, a section of memory is reserved for the instance. Specifically, memory is allocated for the attributes to be contained in the instance. This *memory allocation* contains the attribute definitions for the class as well as values stored in the instance attributes. When we create an account instance, memory is allocated for the instance attributes *account-number*, *current-balance*, and *customer-ss-no*. The data values for these attributes are stored using the private instance method **PopulateAccount**. The instance pointer, anAccount in this example, points to the memory segment that represents the account instance. Figure 6.6 depicts an instance of Account.

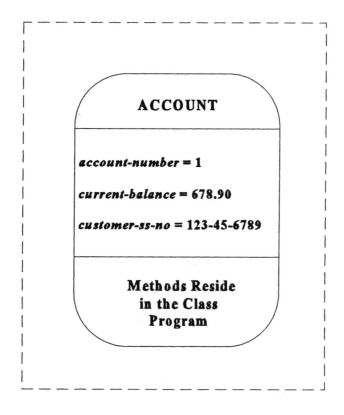

Figure 6.6 An Instance of Account

Similarly, when we create an instance of a subclass, such as CheckingAccount, memory is allocated for the CheckingAccount attribute *lowest-balance*, **and the attributes for the superclass**, Account. In our credit union system when a customer opens a checking account, we need to store the *account-number, customer-ss-no, current-balance*, and *lowest-balance*. The first three attributes are defined in the Account class, and the *lowest-balance* is defined in the CheckingAccount class. When we create an instance of CheckingAccount, a *composite instance*, as shown in Figure 6.7 is created. That is, a section of memory is allocated for the four attributes. The instance method **PopulateAccount** stores values in the first three attributes, while the CheckingAccount method, **PopulateCheckingAccount**, stores the value for *lowest-balance*.

Recall that the instance methods, although they appear to be in each instance, are actually in the class program and are not physically duplicated for each instance. It would be a significant waste of storage to duplicate the method code for each instance we create. Although the code is tied to the instance, it is not physically stored there. We do, however, specify the instance pointer in the INVOKE statement whenever we invoke an instance method, inherited or not.

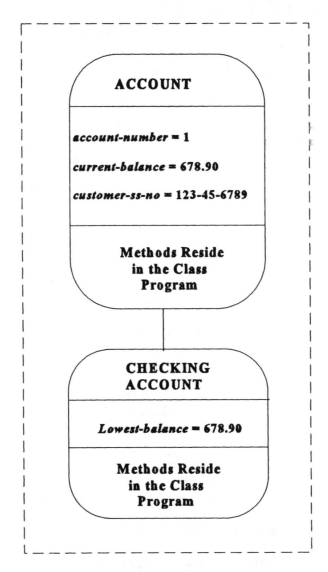

**Figure 6.7 An Instance of <u>Account</u>
and <u>CheckingAccount</u>**

Persistent Instances

The examples in this chapter have not addressed the problem of maintaining an account after it has been opened. For example, when a customer opens a checking account today, we obviously need to retain the account information so that we can post checks and deposits to it in the future. In the example in this chapter, however, when the system stops running, the account and its related data values will disappear because the instance we created exists only in the computer's memory and we have made no provision to retain it.

An instance that exists over time is called a *persistent instance*. In order for our credit union system to be functional, we must provide for persistent instances. We must store account information for future processing. The next chapter deals with this issue in detail.

Destroying Instances

We saw earlier that whenever we create an instance (a checking account, for example), the instance requires that a section of memory be allocated for the attributes. We have not seen, however, what happens to this instance and its related memory allocation when we are finished with it. Suppose, for example, we open a checking account, populate the attributes, and post a check. When the checking account instance is created, we have an instance pointer contained in aCheckingAccount that points to the area of memory containing the instance. Next, let's assume we open a second checking account. We create a second instance and populate the attributes. However, the pointer for the second instance is also in aCheckingAccount. We have erased the pointer to the first instance and thus have lost all contact with it. The memory for the first instance is still allocated, and as far as the system is concerned, it is still in use. However, we have no way to access the first instance or to release the memory that it occupies.

Failing to release this memory could result in our system consuming all of the memory resource as instance after instance is created. Even with a large amount of memory, we will eventually consume all of it as we do processing for our credit union.

When we no longer need an instance, we should erase it in order to release the memory that was allocated. The tentative ANSI-9X standard does not provide for automatic instance deletion. Therefore, we should be aware that our class programs may be required to delete instances that we create to avoid running out of memory. Vendor-specific compilers provide various implementations of instance destruction, but we will not demonstrate these here.

Summary

This chapter has explored the development of subclasses and the invocation of inherited and noninherited methods. We expanded the Account class and then developed class programs for the subclasses CheckingAccount, LoanAccount, and SavingsAccount. We then provided a driver program to invoke the various methods in these classes.

In this chapter, we also described the creation of instances for subclasses. Whenever we create an instance of a subclass, we see that memory is allocated for both superclass and subclass attributes, in effect creating a composite instance.

We also introduced the idea of persistent instances. The next chapter is devoted to this important topic. Finally, we noted the problem associated with the allocation of memory when we create instances and never release the memory that was allocated.

You should now understand how to develop class programs for superclasses and subclasses and how to take advantage of inherited methods.

Key Terms

Client-server	**Inherited methods**	**Private method**
Composite instance	**Memory allocation**	**Public method**
Inherited attributes	**Persistent instances**	**Subclasses**

Review Questions

1.   What attributes are stored in memory for subclass A when an instance is created? Where are the methods stored?

2.   What attributes are stored in memory for superclass A when an instance is created? Where are the methods stored?

3.   What happens to the memory allocated for an instance when the pointer is removed?

Exercises

1.   Design logic (of your own choosing) and add code to the class program for SavingsAccount to maintain a value in the average balance attribute. In your design, you will want to consider how to deal with deposits and withdrawals as well as when (daily, weekly, monthly) to reset the average.

2.   Design and write a class program for a subclass of LoanAccount. Candidate classes are HomeLoan, AutoLoan, BoatLoan, and StudentLoan. Carefully consider which attributes are unique to your subclass and which are inherited from either Account or LoanAccount. Also consider whether methods such as **ComputeInterest** will be inherited or noninherited. Make your design take advantage of inheritance wherever possible.

CLASS DESCRIPTIONS

1. CH6-ACCT is a class program for Account. It is a copy of CH5-ACCT with the additional instance methods ChangeCurrentBalance and TellCustomerSSNo.

Attributes:
```
account-number      PIC 9(5)
customer-ss-no      PIC 9(5)
current-balance     PIC S9(5)V99
```

Factory Method:
```
OpenNewAccount USING account-number, customer-ss-no,
               current-balance
               RETURNING anAccount
```

Instance Methods:
```
#ChangeCurrentBalance       USING current-balance
<private> PopulateAccount USING account-number
                            customer-ss-no, current-balance
TellCurrentBalance          RETURNING current-balance
#TellCustomerSSNo           RETURNING customer-ss-no
```

\# Method added for Chapter 6.

2. CH6-CHEK is a class program for CheckingAccount.

Attribute: `lowest-balance PIC S9(5)V99`

Factory Method:
```
OpenCheckingAccount USING account-number, customer-ss-no,
                    current-balance
                    RETURNING return-data *
```

Instance Methods:
```
ComputeServiceCharge        RETURNING service-charge
<private> PopulateCheckingAccount USING lowest-balance
RecordCheck                 USING amount-of-check, anAccount
RecordDeposit               USING amount-of-deposit, anAccount
TellLowestBalance           RETURNING lowest-balance
```

* Return-data contains return-code and anAccount.

3. CH6-LOAN is a class program for LoanAccount.

Attributes:
```
original-balance    PIC S9(5)V99
interest-rate       PIC 9(2)V99
interest-paid       PIC 9(4)V99
```

Factory Method:
```
OpenLoanAccount USING account-number, customer-ss-no
                original-balance, interest-rate
                RETURNING return-data *
```

Instance Methods:
```
ComputeInterest       RETURNING interest-this-month
<private> PopulateLoanAccount USING original-balance,
          interest-rate.
RecordPayment USING payment-amount RETURNING current-balance
TellInterestPaid       RETURNING interest-paid.
TellInterestRate       RETURNING interest-rate.
TellOriginalBalance    RETURNING original-balance
```

* Return-data contains return-code and anAccount.

4. **CH6-SVGS** is a class program for SavingsAccount.
    Attributes:
```
    interest-earned    PIC 9(5)V99
    average-balance    PIC S9(5)V99
```

Factory Method:
```
OpenSavingsAccount USING account-number, customer-ss-no,
                   current-balance,
                   RETURNING return-data *
```

Instance Methods:
```
ComputeInterest       USING interest-rate
                      RETURNING interest-amount
<private> PopulateSAVINGSAccount USING interest-earned,
          average-balance
RecordDeposit         USING amount-of-deposit
RecordWithdrawal      USING amount-of-withdrawal
TellAverageBalance    RETURNING average-balance
TellInterestEarned    RETURNING interest-earned
```

* Return-data contains return-code and anAccount.

PROGRAM LISTINGS

Account Class Program

```
*    CH6-ACCT is a class program for Account
*    Factory Methods:   OpenNewAccount USING account-number,
*                          customer-ss-no, current-balance
*                       RETURNING anAccount.
*    Instance methods: ChangeCurrentBalance USING current-balance
*                       <private>PopulateAccount USING account-number
*                          customer-ss-no, current-balance.
*                       TellCurrentBalance RETURNING current-balance.
*                       TellCustomerSSNo RETURNING customer-ss-no
*
*    Attributes: account-number  PIC 9(5)
*                customer-ss-no  PIC 9(5)
*                current-balance PIC S9(5)V99
*
*-------------------------------------------------------------
```

```
 1    CLASS-ID. CH6-ACCT
 2          data is private
 3          inherits from Base.
 4
 5    OBJECT SECTION.
 6    CLASS-CONTROL.
 7        Base       is class "Base"
 8        Account    is class "CH6-ACCT".
 9
10    CLASS-OBJECT.
11    OBJECT-STORAGE SECTION.
12
13    *------ Factory Method ---------------------------------
14
15    METHOD-ID. "OpenNewAccount".
16    LINKAGE SECTION.
17    01   account-number-ls       PIC 9(5).
18    01   customer-ss-no-ls       PIC 9(9).
19    01   current-balance-ls      PIC S9(5)V99.
20    01   anAccount          Usage is Object Reference.
21
22    PROCEDURE DIVISION    USING account-number-ls, customer-ss-no-ls
23                            current-balance-ls
24                          RETURNING anAccount.
25        INVOKE Self "New" RETURNING anAccount
26        INVOKE anAccount  "PopulateAccount"
27                          USING account-number-ls, customer-ss-no-ls
28                            current-balance-ls
29        END-INVOKE
30        EXIT METHOD.
31    END METHOD "OpenNewAccount".
32    END CLASS-OBJECT.
33    *------Instance Methods --------------------------------
34    OBJECT.
35    OBJECT-STORAGE SECTION.
36    01  account-info-os.
```

```
37              05    account-number-os       PIC X(5).
38              05    customer-ss-no-os       PIC X(9).
39              05    current-balance-os      PIC S9(5)V99.
40         *-------------------------------------------------------
41         METHOD-ID. "ChangeCurrentBalance".
42         LINKAGE SECTION.
43         01   current-balance-ls      PIC S9(5)V99.
44
45         PROCEDURE DIVISION USING current-balance-ls.
46              MOVE current-balance-ls  to current-balance-os
47              EXIT METHOD.
48         END METHOD "ChangeCurrentBalance".
49         *-------------------------------------------------------
50         METHOD-ID. "PopulateAccount".
51         LINKAGE SECTION.
52         01   account-number-ls       PIC 9(5).
53         01   customer-ss-no-ls       PIC 9(9).
54         01   current-balance-ls      PIC S9(5)V99.
55
56         PROCEDURE DIVISION USING account-number-ls, customer-ss-no-ls
57                                 current-balance-ls.
58              MOVE account-number-ls   TO account-number-os
59              MOVE customer-ss-no-ls   TO customer-ss-no-os
60              MOVE current-balance-ls  TO current-balance-os
61              EXIT METHOD.
62         END METHOD "PopulateAccount".
63         *-------------------------------------------------------
64         METHOD-ID. "TellCurrentBalance".
65         LINKAGE SECTION.
66         01   current-balance-ls  PIC S9(5)V99.
67
68         PROCEDURE DIVISION  RETURNING current-balance-ls.
69              MOVE current-balance-os TO current-balance-ls
70              EXIT METHOD.
71         END METHOD "TellCurrentBalance".
72
73
74         *-------------------------------------------------------
75         METHOD-ID. "TellCustomerSSNo".
76         LINKAGE SECTION.
77         01   customer-ss-no-ls  PIC 9(9).
78
79         PROCEDURE DIVISION  RETURNING customer-ss-no-ls.
80              MOVE customer-ss-no-os TO customer-ss-no-ls
81              EXIT METHOD.
82         END METHOD "TellCustomerSSNo".
83         END OBJECT.
84         END CLASS CH6-ACCT.
85
86
```

Checking Account Class Program

```
*    CH6-CHEK is a class program for CheckingAccount which is a
*       subclass of CH6-ACCT (Account). This class illustrates
*       inherited methods and attributes.
*  Factory Method:    OpenCheckingAccount
*                          USING account-number, customer-ss-no
*                                 current-balance
*                          RETURNING return-data
*  Instance Methods: ComputeServiceCharge
*                          RETURNING service-charge
*                      <private> PopulateCheckingAccount
*                          USING lowest-balance
*                      RecordCheck
*                          USING amount-of-check, anAccount.
*                      RecordDeposit
*                          USING amount-of-deposit, anAccount.
*                      TellLowestBalance RETURNING lowest-balance-ls.
*
*  Attribute: lowest-balance PIC S9(5)V99
*-------------------------------------------------------------
```

```
 1     CLASS-ID.  CH6-CHEK
 2         DATA IS PRIVATE
 3         INHERITS FROM CH6-ACCT.
 4
 5     OBJECT SECTION.
 6     CLASS-CONTROL.
 7         Account               is class "CH6-ACCT"
 8         CheckingAccount       is class "CH6-CHEK".
 9
10     CLASS-OBJECT.
11
12     *------ Factory Methods -------------------------------------
13     METHOD-ID. "OpenCheckingAccount".
14     WORKING-STORAGE SECTION.
15     01  lowest-balance-ws         PIC S9(5)V99.
16     LINKAGE SECTION.
17     01   account-number-ls        PIC 9(5).
18     01   customer-ss-no-ls        PIC 9(9).
19     01   current-balance-ls       PIC S9(5)V99.
20     01   return-data-ls.
21         05   return-code-ls       PIC X(3).
22         05   anAccount        USAGE IS OBJECT REFERENCE.
23
24     PROCEDURE DIVISION USING      account-number-ls
25                                   customer-ss-no-ls
26                                   current-balance-ls
27                        RETURNING return-data-ls.
28         INVOKE Self "OpenNewAccount"
29             USING      account-number-ls
30                        customer-ss-no-ls
31                        current-balance-ls
32             RETURNING  anAccount
33         END-INVOKE
34         MOVE current-balance-ls TO lowest-balance-ws
```

```
35              INVOKE anAccount "PopulateCheckingAccount"
36                   USING  lowest-balance-ws
37              END-INVOKE
38              EXIT METHOD.
39          END METHOD "OpenCheckingAccount".
40          END CLASS-OBJECT.
41
42          *------Instance Methods ---------------------------------------
43
44          OBJECT.
45          OBJECT-STORAGE SECTION.
46          01   checking-account-attributes-os.
47               05  lowest-balance-os       PIC S9(5)V99.
48          *-------------------------------------------------------------
49          METHOD-ID. "ComputeServiceCharge".
50          LINKAGE SECTION.
51          01   service-charge-ls            Pic 9(4)V99.
52          PROCEDURE DIVISION RETURNING service-charge-ls.
53              IF lowest-balance-os < 100.00
54                  MOVE 5.00 to service-charge-ls
55              ELSE
56                  MOVE zeros to service-charge-ls
57              END-IF
58              EXIT METHOD.
59          END METHOD "ComputeServiceCharge".
60          *-------------------------------------------------------------
61          METHOD-ID. "PopulateCheckingAccount".
62          LINKAGE SECTION.
63          01   lowest-balance-ls       PIC 9(5)V99.
64          PROCEDURE DIVISION USING lowest-balance-ls.
65              MOVE lowest-balance-ls TO lowest-balance-os
66              EXIT METHOD.
67          END METHOD "PopulateCheckingAccount".
68          *-------------------------------------------------------------
69          METHOD-ID. "RecordCheck".
70          WORKING-STORAGE SECTION.
71          01   current-balance-ws          PIC S9(5)V99.
72          LINKAGE SECTION.
73          01   amount-of-check-ls          PIC 9(5)V99.
74          01   anAccount         USAGE IS OBJECT REFERENCE.
75
76          PROCEDURE DIVISION USING     amount-of-check-ls, anAccount.
77              INVOKE Self  "TellCurrentBalance"
78                  RETURNING  current-balance-ws
79              END-INVOKE
80              SUBTRACT amount-of-check-ls FROM  current-balance-ws
81              INVOKE Self  "ChangeCurrentBalance"
82                  USING  current-balance-ws
83              END-INVOKE
84              IF current-balance-ws <  lowest-balance-os
85                  MOVE current-balance-ws TO lowest-balance-os
86              END-IF
87              EXIT METHOD.
88          END METHOD "RecordCheck".
89          *-------------------------------------------------------------
90          METHOD-ID. "RecordDeposit".
91          WORKING-STORAGE SECTION.
```

```
92      01  current-balance-ws            PIC S9(5)V99.
93      LINKAGE SECTION.
94      01  amount-of-deposit-ls          PIC 9(5)V99.
95      01  anAccount        USAGE IS OBJECT REFERENCE.
96      PROCEDURE DIVISION USING amount-of-deposit-ls, anAccount.
97
98          INVOKE Self  "TellCurrentBalance"
99              RETURNING  current-balance-ws
100         END-INVOKE
101         ADD amount-of-deposit-ls TO  current-balance-ws
102         INVOKE Self  "ChangeCurrentBalance"
103             USING  current-balance-ws
104         END-INVOKE
105         EXIT METHOD.
106     END METHOD "RecordDeposit".
107     *-------------------------------------------------------
108     METHOD-ID. "TellLowestBalance".
109     LINKAGE SECTION.
110     01  lowest-balance-ls        Pic S9(5)V99.
111     PROCEDURE DIVISION  RETURNING lowest-balance-ls.
112         MOVE lowest-balance-os to lowest-balance-ls
113         EXIT METHOD.
114     END METHOD "TellLowestBalance".
115     END OBJECT.
116
117     END CLASS CH6-CHEK.
```

Loan Account Class Program

```
*  CH6-LOAN is a class program for LoanAccount which is a
*    subclass of CH6-ACCT (Account). This class illustrates
*    inherited methods and attributes.
*  Factory Method:   OpenLoanAccount
*                       USING account-number, customer-ss-no,
*                             original-balance, interest-rate
*                       RETURNING return-data.
*  Instance Methods: ComputeInterest
*                       RETURNING interest-this-month.
*                    <private>PopulateLoanAccount
*                       USING original-balance, interest-rate.
*                    RecordPayment USING payment-amount
*                             RETURNING current-balance.
*                    TellInterestPaid RETURNING interest-paid.
*                    TellInterestRate RETURNING interest-rate.
*                    TellOriginalBalance
*                       RETURNING original-balance.
*
*    Attributes:   original-balance PIC S9(5)V99
*                  interest-rate    PIC 9(2)V99
*                  interest-paid    PIC 9(4)V99
*
*-------------------------------------------------------------
```

```
1      CLASS-ID. CH6-LOAN
2          DATA IS PRIVATE
3          INHERITS FROM CH6-ACCT.
4
5      OBJECT SECTION.
6      CLASS-CONTROL.
7          Account     is class "CH6-ACCT"
8          LoanAccount is class "CH6-LOAN".
9
10     CLASS-OBJECT.
11     OBJECT-STORAGE SECTION.
12
13
14     *------ Factory Method ------------------------------------
15
16     METHOD-ID. "OpenLoanAccount".
17     LINKAGE SECTION.
18     01   account-number-ls          PIC 9(5).
19     01   customer-ss-no-ls          PIC 9X(9).
20     01   original-balance-ls        PIC S9(5)V99.
21     01   interest-rate-ls           PIC 9(2)V99.
22     01   interest-paid-ls           PIC 9(4)V99.
23     01   return-data-ls.
24          05   return-code-ls        PIC X(3).
25          05   anAccount     USAGE IS OBJECT REFERENCE.
26
27
28     PROCEDURE DIVISION  USING account-number-ls, customer-ss-no-ls
29                               original-balance-ls, interest-rate-ls
30                         RETURNING return-data-ls.
```

```
31              INVOKE Self "OpenNewAccount"
32                          USING account-number-ls, customer-ss-no-ls,
33                              original-balance-ls
34                          RETURNING anAccount
35          END-INVOKE
36          INVOKE anAccount "PopulateLoanAccount"
37                          USING original-balance-ls, interest-rate-ls
38          END-INVOKE
39          EXIT METHOD.
40      END METHOD "OpenLoanAccount".
41      END CLASS-OBJECT.
42      OBJECT.
43      OBJECT-STORAGE SECTION.
44      01  loan-attributes-os.
45          05  original-balance-os     PIC S9(5)V99.
46          05  interest-rate-os        PIC 9(2)V99.
47          05  interest-paid-os        PIC 9(4)V99.
48      *-----------------------------------------------------
49      METHOD-ID. "ComputeInterest".
50      WORKING-STORAGE SECTION.
51      01  current-balance-ws          PIC S9(5)V99.
52
53      LINKAGE SECTION.
54      01  interest-this-month-ls      PIC 9(4)V99.
55
56      PROCEDURE DIVISION RETURNING interest-this-month-ls.
57          INVOKE Self  "TellCurrentBalance"
58              RETURNING current-balance-ws
59          END-INVOKE
60          COMPUTE interest-this-month-ls ROUNDED =
61              current-balance-ws *
62              ((interest-rate-os/100)) / 12
63          END-COMPUTE
64          EXIT METHOD.
65      END METHOD "ComputeInterest".
66      *-----------------------------------------------------
67      METHOD-ID. "PopulateLoanAccount".
68      LINKAGE SECTION.
69      * LOAN Attributes
70      01  original-balance-ls         PIC S9(5)V99.
71      01  interest-rate-ls            PIC 9(2)V99.
72      PROCEDURE DIVISION USING original-balance-ls, interest-rate-ls.
73          MOVE original-balance-ls TO original-balance-os
74          MOVE interest-rate-ls    TO interest-rate-os
75          MOVE ZEROS               TO interest-paid-os
76          EXIT METHOD.
77      END METHOD "PopulateLoanAccount".
78
79
80
81      *-----------------------------------------------------
82      METHOD-ID. "RecordPayment".
83      WORKING-STORAGE SECTION.
84      01  interest-this-month-ws      PIC 9(4)V99.
85      01  current-balance-ws          PIC S9(5)V99.
86
87      LINKAGE SECTION.
```

```
 88        01   payment-amount-ls            PIC 9(5)V99.
 89        01   current-balance-ls           PIC S9(5)V99.
 90
 91        PROCEDURE DIVISION USING       payment-amount-ls
 92                          RETURNING current-balance-ls.
 93            INVOKE Self  "ComputeInterest"
 94                RETURNING interest-this-month-ws
 95            END-INVOKE
 96            INVOKE Self  "TellCurrentBalance"
 97                RETURNING current-balance-ws
 98            END-INVOKE
 99            COMPUTE current-balance-ws ROUNDED = current-balance-ws -
100                (payment-amount-ls - interest-this-month-ws)
101            INVOKE Self  "ChangeCurrentBalance"
102                USING current-balance-ws
103            END-INVOKE
104            COMPUTE interest-paid-os =
105                interest-paid-os + interest-this-month-ws
106            END-COMPUTE
107            MOVE current-balance-ws TO current-balance-ls
108            EXIT METHOD.
109        END METHOD "RecordPayment".
110        *-------------------------------------------------------
111        METHOD-ID. "TellInterestPaid".
112        LINKAGE SECTION.
113        01   interest-paid-ls             Pic 9(4)V99.
114
115        PROCEDURE DIVISION RETURNING interest-paid-ls.
116            MOVE interest-paid-os TO interest-paid-ls
117            EXIT METHOD.
118        END METHOD "TellInterestPaid".
119
120
121        *-------------------------------------------------------
122        METHOD-ID. "TellInterestRate".
123        LINKAGE SECTION.
124        01  .interest-rate-ls             Pic 9(4)V99.
125
126        PROCEDURE DIVISION RETURNING interest-rate-ls.
127            MOVE interest-rate-os TO interest-rate-ls
128            EXIT METHOD.
129        END METHOD "TellInterestRate".
130        *-------------------------------------------------------
131        METHOD-ID. "TellOriginalBalance".
132        LINKAGE SECTION.
133        01   original-balance-ls          Pic S9(5)V99.
134
135        PROCEDURE DIVISION  RETURNING original-balance-ls.
136            MOVE original-balance-os to original-balance-ls
137            EXIT METHOD.
138        END METHOD "TellOriginalBalance".
139        END OBJECT.
140
141        END CLASS CH6-LOAN.
142
143
           *-------------------------------------------------------
```

Savings Account Class Program

```
     *   CH6-SVGS is a class program for SavingsAccount which is a
     *     subclass of CH6-ACCT (Account).
     * Factory Method:   OpenSavingsAccount
     *                      USING account-number, customer-ss-no,
     *                            current-balance
     *                      RETURNING return-data.
     * Instance Methods: ComputeInterest USING interest-rate
     *                              RETURNING interest-amount.
     *                     <private>PopulateSavingsAccount
     *                        USING interest-earned, average-balance.
     *                     RecordDeposit USING amount-of-deposit.
     *                     RecordWithdrawal USING amount-of-withdrawal.
     *                     TellAverageBalance RETURNING average-balance.
     *                     TellInterestEarned RETURNING interest-earned.
     *
     *    Attributes:  interest-earned PIC 9(5)V99
     *                 average-balance PIC S9(5)V99
     *
     *-------------------------------------------------------------
```

```
 1      CLASS-ID. CH6-SVGS
 2         DATA IS PRIVATE
 3         INHERITS FROM CH6-ACCT.
 4
 5      OBJECT SECTION.
 6      CLASS-CONTROL.
 7         Account         is class "CH6-ACCT"
 8         SavingsAccount  is class "CH6-SVGS".
 9
10      CLASS-OBJECT.
11      OBJECT-STORAGE SECTION.
12
13      *------ Factory Method ----------------------------------------
14
15      METHOD-ID. "OpenSavingsAccount".
16      WORKING-STORAGE SECTION.
17      01   interest-earned-ws        PIC S9(5)V99.
18      01   average-balance-ws        PIC S9(5)V99.
19
20      LINKAGE SECTION.
21      01   account-number-ls         PIC 9(5).
22      01   customer-ss-no-ls         PIC 9(9).
23      01   current-balance-ls        PIC S9(5)V99.
24      01   return-data-ls.
25         05   return-code-ls         PIC X(3).
26         05   anAccount          USAGE IS OBJECT REFERENCE.
27
28      PROCEDURE DIVISION  USING account-number-ls, customer-ss-no-ls
29                              current-balance-ls
30                          RETURNING return-data-ls.
31         INVOKE Self "OpenNewAccount"
32                          USING account-number-ls, customer-ss-no-ls,
33                              current-balance-ls
34                          RETURNING anAccount
```

```
35            END-INVOKE
36            MOVE ZEROS TO interest-earned-ws
37                          average-balance-ws
38            INVOKE anAccount "PopulateSavingsAccount"
39                          USING interest-earned-ws, average-balance-ws
40            END-INVOKE
41            EXIT METHOD.
42         END METHOD "OpenSavingsAccount".
43         END CLASS-OBJECT.
44         OBJECT.
45         OBJECT-STORAGE SECTION.
46         01   savings-account-attributes-os.
47              05   interest-earned-os        PIC 9(5)V99.
48              05   average-balance-os        PIC S9(5)V99.
49
50         *------------------------------------------------------------
51         METHOD-ID. "ComputeInterest".
52         LINKAGE SECTION.
53         01   interest-amount-ls             PIC 9(4)V99.
54         01   interest-rate-ls               PIC 9(2)V99.
55         PROCEDURE DIVISION USING interest-rate-ls
56                 RETURNING interest-amount-ls.
57              COMPUTE interest-amount-ls =
58                  (interest-rate-ls/12)/100 * average-balance-os
59              END-COMPUTE.
60              EXIT METHOD..
61         END METHOD "ComputeInterest".
62
63
64         *------------------------------------------------------------
65         METHOD-ID. "PopulateSavingsAccount".
66         LINKAGE SECTION.
67         * CheckingAccount Attributes
68         01   interest-earned-ls      PIC 9(5)V99.
69         01   average-balance-ls      PIC S9(5)V99.
70         PROCEDURE DIVISION USING interest-earned-ls, average-balance-ls.
71              MOVE interest-earned-ls TO interest-earned-os
72              MOVE average-balance-ls TO average-balance-os
73              EXIT METHOD.
74         END METHOD "PopulateSavingsAccount".
75         *------------------------------------------------------------
76         METHOD-ID. "RecordDeposit".
77         WORKING-STORAGE SECTION.
78         01   current-balance-ws             PIC S9(5)V99.
79
80         LINKAGE SECTION.
81         01   amount-of-deposit-ls           PIC 9(5)V99.
82
83         PROCEDURE DIVISION USING amount-of-deposit-ls.
84              INVOKE Self  "TellCurrentBalance"
85                  RETURNING current-balance-ws
86              END-INVOKE
87              ADD amount-of-deposit-ls TO  current-balance-ws
88              INVOKE Self  "ChangeCurrentBalance"
89                  USING  current-balance-ws
90              END-INVOKE
91              EXIT METHOD.
```

```
 92         END METHOD "RecordDeposit".
 93         *-------------------------------------------------------
 94         METHOD-ID. "RecordWithdrawal".
 95         WORKING-STORAGE SECTION.
 96         01  current-balance-ws          PIC S9(5)V99.
 97
 98         LINKAGE SECTION.
 99         01  amount-of-withdrawal-ls     PIC 9(5)V99.
100
101         PROCEDURE DIVISION USING amount-of-withdrawal-ls.
102             INVOKE Self  "TellCurrentBalance"
103                 RETURNING  current-balance-ws
104             END-INVOKE
105             SUBTRACT amount-of-withdrawal-ls FROM current-balance-ws
106             INVOKE Self  "ChangeCurrentBalance"
107                 USING  current-balance-ws
108             END-INVOKE
109             EXIT METHOD.
110         END METHOD "RecordWithdrawal".
111         *-------------------------------------------------------
112         METHOD-ID. "TellAverageBalance".
113         LINKAGE SECTION.
114         01  average-balance-ls          PIC S9(5)V99.
115
116         PROCEDURE DIVISION  RETURNING average-balance-ls.
117             MOVE average-balance-os to average-balance-ls.
118             EXIT METHOD..
119         END METHOD "TellAverageBalance".
120
121         *-------------------------------------------------------
122         METHOD-ID. "TellInterestEarned".
123         LINKAGE SECTION.
124         01  interest-earned-ls      PIC 9(5)V99.
125         PROCEDURE DIVISION  RETURNING interest-earned-ls.
126             MOVE interest-earned-os to interest-earned-ls
127             EXIT METHOD.
128         END METHOD "TellInterestEarned".
129         END OBJECT.
130         END CLASS CH6-SVGS.
```

Driver Program

```
*   CH6-PRG1 is a procedural COBOL program used to illustrate
*     the invocation of methods in the Account superclass and
*       in subclasses CheckingAccount, LoanAccount, SavingsAccount
*-------------------------------------------------------------
```

```
 1      PROGRAM-ID. CH6-PRG1.
 2      *-------------------------------------------------------------
 3      CLASS-CONTROL.
 4          Account          IS CLASS "CH6-ACCT"
 5          CheckingAccount is class "CH6-CHEK"
 6          LoanAccount      IS CLASS "CH6-LOAN"
 7          SavingsAccount  is class "CH6-SVGS".
 8
 9      WORKING-STORAGE SECTION.
10          01  aCheckingAccount        USAGE IS OBJECT REFERENCE.
11          01  aLoanAccount            USAGE IS OBJECT REFERENCE.
12          01  aSavingsAccount         USAGE IS OBJECT REFERENCE.
13          01  return-data-ws.
14              05  return-code-ws          PIC X(3).
15              05  anAccount-ws    USAGE IS OBJECT REFERENCE.
16          01  service-charge-ws       PIC 9(4)V99.
17          01  amount-of-check-ws      PIC 9(5)V99.
18          01  amount-of-deposit-ws    PIC 9(5)V99.
19          01  interest-amount-ws      PIC 9(4)V99.
20
21      *  Account Attributes
22          01  account-number-ws       PIC 9(5).
23          01  customer-ss-no-ws       PIC 9(9).
24          01  current-balance-ws      PIC S9(5)V99.
25
26      *  Checking Account Attributes
27          01  lowest-balance-ws       PIC S9(5)V99.
28
29      *  LoanAccount Attributes
30          01  original-balance-ws     PIC S9(5)V99.
31          01  interest-rate-ws        PIC 9(2)V99.
32          01  interest-paid-ws        PIC 9(4)V99.
33          01  interest-this-month-ws  PIC 9(4)V99.
34          01  payment-amount-ws       PIC 9(5)V99.
35
36      *  Savings Account Attributes
37          01  interest-earned-ws      PIC 9(5)V99.
38          01  average-balance-ws      PIC S9(5)V99.
39
40      PROCEDURE DIVISION.
41          PERFORM CREATE-ACCOUNTS
42          PERFORM GET-AND-DISPLAY-BALANCES
43          PERFORM EXERCISE-CHECKING-METHODS
44          PERFORM EXERCISE-LOAN-METHODS
45          PERFORM EXERCISE-SAVINGS-METHODS
46          STOP RUN.
47
48      CREATE-ACCOUNTS.
49      * Open a Checking Account
```

```
50        MOVE 1           TO   account-number-ws
51        MOVE 123456789 TO   customer-ss-no-ws
52        MOVE 678.90      TO   current-balance-ws
53        INVOKE CheckingAccount "OpenCheckingAccount"
54            USING        account-number-ws, customer-ss-no-ws,
55                         current-balance-ws
56            RETURNING    return-data-ws
57        END-INVOKE
58        SET aCheckingAccount TO anAccount-ws
59   * Open a Loan Account
60        MOVE 2           TO   account-number-ws
61        MOVE 234567890 TO   customer-ss-no-ws
62        MOVE 123.45      TO   original-balance-ws
63        MOVE 7.25        TO   interest-rate-ws
64        INVOKE LoanAccount "OpenLoanAccount"
65            USING        account-number-ws, customer-ss-no-ws,
66                         original-balance-ws, interest-rate-ws
67            RETURNING    return-data-ws
68        END-INVOKE
69        SET aLoanAccount TO anAccount-ws
70   * Open a Savings Account
71        MOVE 3           TO   account-number-ws
72        MOVE 345678901 TO   customer-ss-no-ws
73        MOVE 345.67      TO   current-balance-ws
74        INVOKE SavingsAccount "OpenSavingsAccount"
75            USING        account-number-ws, customer-ss-no-ws,
76                         current-balance-ws
77            RETURNING    return-data-ws
78        END-INVOKE
79        SET aSavingsAccount TO anAccount-ws.
80
81
82    GET-AND-DISPLAY-BALANCES.
83        INVOKE aCheckingAccount "TellCurrentBalance"
84            RETURNING current-balance-ws
85        END-INVOKE
86        DISPLAY "The Checking Balance is: ", current-balance-ws
87        END-DISPLAY
88        INVOKE aLoanAccount "TellCurrentBalance"
89            RETURNING current-balance-ws
90        END-INVOKE
91        DISPLAY "The Loan Balance is: ", current-balance-ws
92        END-DISPLAY
93        INVOKE aSavingsAccount "TellCurrentBalance"
94            RETURNING current-balance-ws
95        END-INVOKE
96        DISPLAY "The Savings Balance is: ", current-balance-ws
97        END-DISPLAY.
98
99    EXERCISE-CHECKING-METHODS.
100        DISPLAY "Now Exercising Checking Methods......"
101        INVOKE aCheckingAccount "ComputeServiceCharge"
102            RETURNING service-charge-ws
103        END-INVOKE
104        DISPLAY "The Service Charge Amount is: ", service-charge-ws
105
106        MOVE 50.00 TO amount-of-check-ws
```

```
107          INVOKE aCheckingAccount "RecordCheck"
108              USING amount-of-check-ws, aCheckingAccount
109          END-INVOKE
110          INVOKE aCheckingAccount "TellCurrentBalance"
111              RETURNING current-balance-ws
112          END-INVOKE
113          DISPLAY "The Checking Balance After a $50 check is: ",
114              current-balance-ws
115          END-DISPLAY
116
117          INVOKE aCheckingAccount "TellLowestBalance"
118              RETURNING lowest-balance-ws
119          END-INVOKE
120          DISPLAY "The Checking Lowest Balance is: ",
121              lowest-balance-ws
122          END-DISPLAY
123
124      EXERCISE-LOAN-METHODS.
125          DISPLAY "Now Exercising Loan Methods......"
126          MOVE 100.00 TO payment-amount-ws
127          INVOKE aLoanAccount  "RecordPayment"
128              USING payment-amount-ws
129              RETURNING current-balance-ws
130          END-INVOKE
131          DISPLAY "The Balance after the payment is: ",
132              current-balance-ws
133          END-DISPLAY
134          INVOKE aLoanAccount "TellInterestPaid"
135              RETURNING interest-paid-ws
136          END-INVOKE
137          DISPLAY "The interest paid is", interest-paid-ws
138          END-DISPLAY
139
140
141      EXERCISE-SAVINGS-METHODS.
142          DISPLAY "Now Exercising Savings Methods......"
143          MOVE 100.00 TO amount-of-deposit-ws
144          INVOKE aSavingsAccount  "RecordDeposit"
145              USING amount-of-deposit-ws
146          END-INVOKE
147          INVOKE aSavingsAccount "TellCurrentBalance"
148              RETURNING current-balance-ws
149          END-INVOKE
150          DISPLAY "The Balance after $100 deposit is: ",
151              current-balance-ws
152          END-DISPLAY
153
154          MOVE 7.25 TO interest-rate-ws
155          INVOKE aSavingsAccount "ComputeInterest"
156              USING interest-rate-ws
157              RETURNING interest-amount-ws
158          END-INVOKE
159          DISPLAY "The Amount of Interest is: ", interest-amount-ws
160          END-DISPLAY
161
162          INVOKE aSavingsAccount "TellAverageBalance"
163              RETURNING average-balance-ws
```

```
164        END-INVOKE
165        DISPLAY "The Average Balance is: ",
166            average-balance-ws
167        END-DISPLAY
168
169    *-------------------------------------------------------------
170
```

CHAPTER 7:

Data Management

Object-oriented systems are good examples of client-server design. We said earlier that an OO system provides system services through methods that are invoked. The invoking program is really a client—a requestor of some service. The class owning the method being invoked is a server—the service provider. In this chapter, we will add data management classes to provide data storage and retrieval services.

Chapters 5 and 6 developed the problem domain classes for Account, CheckingAccount, LoanAccount, and SavingsAccount. In this chapter, one new problem domain class, Customer, will be introduced. This chapter, however, deals primarily with the design of the data management classes indicated in Figure 7.1. These new classes provide data management services to the problem domain classes, giving the credit union system the capability of storing account and customer information for later retrieval and processing.

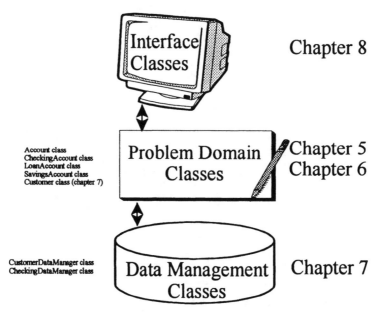

Figure 7.1   Class Layer Diagram

We will develop two data management classes, CheckingDataManager and CustomerDataManager. CheckingDataManager will be designed to store and retrieve checking account data, and CustomerDataManager will store and retrieve customer information.

In Chapter 6, we invoked methods that created instances of all three types of accounts. However, these instances disappeared when the programs stopped running. The account information was not saved so that it could be later retrieved for subsequent processing. The instances were temporary (i.e. *dynamic instances*). However, for real business information systems, we need to be able to store and retrieve this information; we need *persistent instances*. This chapter centers on the creation, storage, and retrieval of persistent instances. We continue with the credit union system by storing information for checking accounts and customers.

At the end of the chapter, you should have a good understanding of how to work with persistent instances and how to design files for storing instance data. This will enable you to develop meaningful business information systems that maintain data.

Why Have Persistent Instances?

In previous chapters, we created dynamic instances. The instances that were created disappeared as soon as the program ended; none of the data was saved to secondary storage. The accounts ceased to exist once the program stopped running. We took this somewhat simplistic approach to give you an introduction to Object COBOL concepts, without the complexity of dealing with files. However, in the real world this would never work.

When a customer opens an account, we want to access the account information in the future. We will need to post transactions to the account, produce account statements, and do additional account-related processing. We want the instances to be persistent. Persistent instances do not disappear when the programs stop running. Instead, the instance data are stored in a file or database.

There are many ways to have persistent instances. The instance can be stored in an object database, a relational database, an indexed file, or a sequential file. The instance can be stored in the same way as we store any other record. Today, many organizations are storing instances in relational databases. In the near future, object databases may well become the norm, but for now, relational databases dominate. Thus, for our discussion, we will create persistent instances by storing them in files that could easily be implemented using a relational database.

Persistent instances present some interesting problems. However, the beauty of object programming is that, should we change the way the files are stored—for example, from flat files to a relational database—the changes are transparent to the client (provided we avoid changing the method interfaces). The physical implementation details are encapsulated in the data management classes. They are hidden from the client.

FILE DESIGN FOR PERSISTENT INSTANCES

The first question to be asked with regard to persistent instances is: Which instances should be persistent? Generally, factors such as the need to retrieve data at a later time and whether other programs/instances share the data help determine whether or not the instances need to be persistent. Once we decide which instances are persistent, we must decide how to store them.

In previous chapters, we developed class programs for Account, CheckingAccount, LoanAccount, and SavingsAccount. The object model representing those classes, shown again in Figure 7.2, will now be the basis for determining the file design for storing the instances. Instances can be mapped into files in the following two ways:

- Each class becomes a file.
- Only subclasses become files.

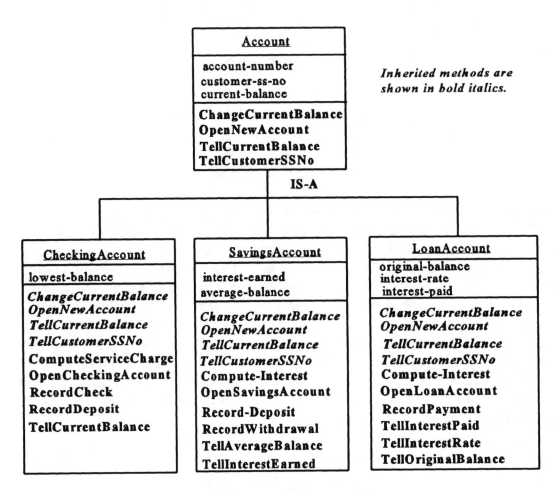

Figure 7.2   Object Model

In either case, attributes become fields and instances become records. However, the manner in which the attributes are stored varies, especially when superclasses and subclasses are introduced. Let's explore each of these options for file design given our object model.

With the first option, each class represented in an object model is translated into a file. The attributes become fields and instances become records. Figure 7.3 illustrates this file design.

Filename:	Account		
Fields:	*account-number*	*customer-ss-no*	*current-balance*
Sample Records:	1234	111-22-3333	$678.89
	2768	222-22-2222	$789.00
	4321	333-22-1111	$110.01
	4399	333-22-1111	$1,999.99
	4431	444-33-2222	$342.99
	4444	111-22-3333	$500.00

Filename:	CheckingAccount			
Fields:	*lowest-balance*	*account-number*	*customer-ss-no*	*current-balance*
Sample Records:	$100.00	1234	111-22-3333	$678.89
	$35.00	4321	333-22-1111	$110.01

Filename:	SavingsAccount				
Fields:	*interest-earned*	*average-balance*	*account-number*	*customer-ss-no*	*current-balance*
Sample Records:	$10.32	$655.00	2768	222-22-2222	$789.00
	$3.56	$1500.00	4399	333-22-1111	$1,999.99

Filename:	LoanAccount					
Fields:	*original-balance*	*interest-rate*	*interest-paid*	*account-number*	*customer-ss-no*	*current-balance*
Sample Records:	$5,000.00	8.5%	$333.23	4431	444-33-2222	$342.99
	$2,000.00	10.0%	$100.00	4444	111-22-3333	$500.00

Filename = ClassName
Field = Attribute
Record = Instance

Figure 7.3   Each Class Becomes a File

The fields shown in italics are inherited from Account. What is wrong with the file design in Figure 7.3? That's right—the *account-number*, *customer-ss-no*, and *current-balance* are duplicated for each type of account. For example, let's suppose we have a CheckingAccount with *account-number* 1234, *customer-ss-no* of 111-22-3333, *current-balance* of $678.99, and a *lowest-balance* of $100. Where is that information stored? As shown in Figure 7.3, the *account-number, customer-ss-no, current-balance,* and *lowest-balance* would all be stored in the CheckingAccount file. But the *account-number, customer-ss-no,* and *current-balance* would also be stored in the Account file. Data redundancy is a problem! Remember from the specifications given earlier: every account has a unique account number; a customer may have all three types of accounts with three different account numbers. Every time we have to change the *current-balance* for the <u>CheckingAccount</u> we also have to change the *current-balance* for the <u>Account</u>. Because of the data redundancy problem, we can quickly conclude that the file design in Figure 7.3 is not the best possible solution.

Another potential solution is shown in Figure 7.4. Here we have not duplicated *current-balance* and *customer-ss-no* in the subclass files. These values now reside only in the superclass file for <u>Account</u>. Whenever a subclass needs one of these values, they will simply invoke a method to retrieve the value from the corresponding account record.

Filename:	<u>Account</u>		
Fields:	*account-number*	*customer-ss-no*	*current-balance*
Sample Records:	1234	111-22-3333	$678.89
	2768	222-22-2222	$789.00
	4321	333-22-1111	$110.01
	4399	333-22-1111	$1,999.99
	4431	444-33-2222	$342.99
	4444	111-22-3333	$500.00

Filename:	<u>CheckingAccount</u>	
Fields:	*lowest-balance*	*account-number*
Sample Records:	$100.00	1234
	$35.00	4321

Filename:	<u>SavingsAccount</u>		
Fields:	*interest-earned*	*average-balance*	*account-number*
Sample Records:	$10.32	$655.00	2768
	$3.56	$1500.00	4399

Filename:	<u>LoanAccount</u>			
Fields:	*original-balance*	*interest-rate*	*interest-paid*	*account-number*
Sample Records:	$5,000.00	8.5%	$333.23	4431
	$2,000.00	10.0%	$100.00	4444

Filename = Class Name
Field = Attribute
Record = Instance

Figure 7.4   A Second Possible File Design

The second solution stores the *current-balance, customer-ss-no,* and *account-number* in <u>Account</u>. Each subclass record contains its unique attributes, plus *account-number*. We are storing *account-number* so that we can find the matching <u>Account</u>. For example, if we have only the *lowest-balance* in the <u>CheckingAccount</u>, how would we know that it belongs to <u>Account</u> 1234? We must store the *account-number* for each subclass instance so that we can find its parent. Is the storage of account number in each of the subclass records a form of data redundancy? In a way, yes. But in this case, it is necessary to link the subclasses to the parent account. If we could avoid storing *account-number* more than once we would, but here we cannot.

Using this file design, if we wanted to add a security code, we would simply add it to the Account class. The subclasses are not affected, yet they will have access to those data through methods provided in the Account class. Should we need to know the current balance for a LoanAccount, for example, we simply send the following message:

```
INVOKE aLoanAccount "TELLCURRENTBALANCE"
      RETURNING Current-balance
```
                           or
```
INVOKE anAccount "TELLCURRENTBALANCE" RETURNING Current-balance
```

The first message to LoanAccount will actually be forwarded to the superclass Account because of inheritance. In the second example, the message is sent directly to the Account class. In both cases, we assume that the appropriate instance pointer is used (i.e., aLoanAccount or anAccount).

This file design seems to be appropriate and would work well for this application. Data redundancy is minimized, and access is provided to all pertinent data. However, we need to explore one more option.

The last option is to create a file for each subclass but not for the superclass. We would then include all of the superclass attributes in each subclass file. In our example, we would have files for CheckingAccount, LoanAccount, and SavingsAccount, but not for the superclass Account.   This approach is shown in Figure 7.5.

Filename:	CheckingAccount			
Fields:	*lowest-balance*	*account-number*	*customer-ss-no*	*current-balance*
Sample Records:	$100.00	1234	111-22-3333	$678.89
	$35.00	4321	333-22-1111	$110.01

Filename:	SavingsAccount				
Fields:	*interest-earned*	*average-balance*	*account-number*	*customer-ss-no*	*current-balance*
Sample Records:	$10.32	$655.00	2768	222-22-2222	$789.00
	$3.56	$1500.00	4399	333-22-1111	$1,999.99

Filename:	LoanAccount					
Fields:	*original-balance*	*interest-rate*	*interest-paid*	*account-number*	*customer-ss-no*	*current-balance*
Sample Records:	$5,000.00	8.5%	$333.23	4431	444-33-2222	$342.99
	$2,000.00	10.0%	$100.00	4444	111-22-3333	$500.00

Filename = Class Name
Field = Attribute
Record = Instance

Figure 7.5 Each Subclass Becomes a File

The design in Figure 7.5 eliminates the data redundancy problem in Figure 7.3. Now, if we have a CheckingAccount with account number 1234, *customer-ss-no* of 111-22-3333, *current-balance* of $678.89, and a *lowest-balance* of $100, all the information is stored in the CheckingAccount file. Is this the best file design? In this case, it probably is. Each type of account owned by a customer would have a unique account number. For example, customer 111-22-3333's checking account number is 1234, but its loan account number is 4444. Thus, we gain nothing by treating the Account class as a separate file. In fact, by treating each subclass as a file, we have eliminated storing *account-number* more than once as shown in Figure 7.4.

For our credit union application, all of the file designs presented would work. However, we are going to use the file design shown in Figure 7.5 for a couple of reasons. First, it is simple: one less file is used, and data redundancy is eliminated. Second, this alternative generally provides faster data access because searching is not necessary to get information about an Account. We will require only one disk access to retrieve all of the account information. Finally, this choice illustrates the separation of the file design from the classes themselves. As you will see later, the file design is completely hidden from the clients of the data management classes. Throughout the remainder of the book, we will use the file design and will implement it as indexed sequential (ISAM) files.

Problem Domain Classes

Each of the four class programs you have seen so far—Account, CheckingAccount, SavingsAccount, and LoanAccount—will require new methods and modification to the existing methods in order to accommodate persistent instances. However, and most importantly, the existing method interfaces will not change. This is a necessary requirement of object programming. Once the interface is established, it should never be changed—even if we add persistent instances using data management classes! Let's start with the Account class.

The Account class, originally developed in Chapter 5 and expanded in Chapter 6, is also used in this chapter and the next. In fact, the Account class program from Chapter 6 (CH6-ACCT) is used in this chapter, with the addition of one new instance method, **TellAccountNumber**. The same class program is used in the next chapter without modification. This is an excellent example of class reuse. It also illustrates how OO facilitates maintenance. We are making significant changes to the credit union system, yet one of the key problem domain class programs will remain untouched!

The CheckingAccount class, developed in the previous chapter, will require some modification. Specifically, two new methods have been added: **CloseCheckingAccount** and **RetrieveCheckingAccount**. Three existing methods are modified: **OpenCheckingAccount**, **RecordCheck**, and **RecordDeposit**. The updated class program for CheckingAccount (CH7-CHEK) is listed at the end of the chapter with the modifications boldfaced.

The first change to note in CheckingAccount is the inclusion of the CheckingDataManager class. This is a new data management class added to accommodate the storage of CheckingAccount instances. The modified methods— **OpenCheckingAccount**, **RecordCheck**, and **RecordDeposit**— have been changed to INVOKE methods in <u>CheckingDataManager</u>. **RetrieveCheckingAccount** has been added so that a specific checking account can be retrieved from the file via the <u>CheckingDataManager</u>. To the client, the manner of retrieval is hidden. The client program simply invokes **RetrieveCheckingAccount**.

The second new method, **CloseCheckingAccount** has been added to delete accounts from a file. Again, the manner in which the deletion occurs is hidden from the client using the method. The execution of these new methods will be demonstrated later.

Next, we are going to develop a <u>Customer</u> class whose responsibility is to maintain information about the customer, such as social security number and name. The <u>Customer</u> class makes the credit union system more realistic and also illustrates the use of a class outside a strict inheritance relationship. Remember from Figure 7.2 that all of the classes so far have existed in the **Is-a** relationship. The revised object model, which now includes the <u>Customer</u> class, is shown in Figure 7.6. The object model is read as "a Customer Owns an Account," illustrating the relationship between a customer and their account.

The class program for <u>Customer</u> is listed at the end of the chapter. This class has two attributes: *customer-ss-no* and *customer-name*. It has two factory methods: **CreateNewCustomer** and **RetrieveCustomer**. It also has four public instance methods: **ChangeCustomerName**, **RemoveCustomer**, **TellCustomerSSNo**, and **TellCustomerName**. In addition, this class has the somewhat familiar private method, **PopulateCustomer**. The interfaces for these methods are shown in the Class Descriptions section at the end of the chapter.

THE CHECKINGDATAMANAGER CLASS

In this section, we present the <u>CheckingDataManager</u> class, which will be used to create persistent instances. First, we'll look at the code for the class itself; then, we'll see how the <u>CheckingAccount</u> class uses it to store the instance data.

<u>CheckingDataManager</u> contains a section that may look very familiar to you: the FILE-CONTROL section. This section specifies the type of file (indexed), the name of the file (CH7-CHKG.DAT), and the name of the key field (*account-number-fs*).

```
FILE-CONTROL.
    SELECT Checking-File ASSIGN TO "CH7-CHKG.DAT"
        ORGANIZATION IS INDEXED
        ACCESS IS RANDOM
        RECORD KEY IS account-number-fs.
```

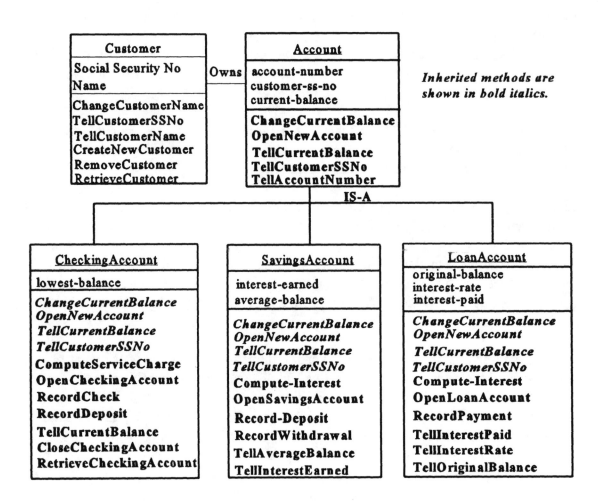

Figure 7.6 Updated Object Model

We will also add a FILE SECTION where we describe the checking record and its fields: *account-number-fs, customer-ss-no-fs, current-balance-fs,* and *lowest-balance-fs.*

```
FILE SECTION.
FD checking-file.
01 checking-record.
    05   account-number-fs        PIC 9(5).
    05   customer-ss-no-fs        PIC 9(9).
    05   current-balance-fs       PIC S9(5)v99.
    05   lowest-balance-fs        PIC S9(5)v99.
```

The remaining methods necessary for storing the instances, such as **StoreRecord**, do not require any knowledge beyond what you already have. Rather than explain each of the methods, let's look at the implementation of the system, such as opening an account and recording a check, and explain the process of using the new CheckingDataManager class.

To illustrate the use of the CheckingDataManager, a driver program, plus CheckingAccount and Account class programs, will be used. Please refer to each of these programs listed at the end of the chapter. The methods **OpenCheckingAccount** and **RetrieveCheckingAccount** will be discussed in some detail below.

The object interaction diagram (OID) for **OpenCheckingAccount** is shown in Figure 7.7. The driver program invokes **OpenCheckingAccount**, which, in turn, invokes **OpenNewAccount** (steps 1 through 5 in Figure 7.7). These steps are the same as illustrated in earlier chapters; the first new step is number 6. Here, CheckingAccount invokes **StoreRecord** in CheckingDataManager. The **StoreRecord** method is listed in Figure 7.8. It is responsible for taking the instance stored in primary memory (i.e., a dynamic instance) and storing it on secondary storage (i.e., persistent instance). To do this, **StoreRecord** uses the instance pointer (anAccount) passed to it to find the account number, the customer social security number, the current balance, and the lowest balance. This information is found by invoking methods in Account and CheckingAccount to return that information (see steps 7 through 10 in Figure 7.7). The information is then written to a file—in this case, an ISAM file.

There is an important question to consider here: Why doesn't CheckingAccount pass all the attributes to **StoreRecord** rather than just the instance pointer anAccount? The answer is simple and yet important. In the future, the attributes of CheckingAccount may change. For example, the credit union may decide to start paying interest on checking accounts. If the interface design calls for CheckingAccount to pass the attribute list to CheckingDataManager, then the interface for **StoreRecord**, among others, would have to be modified to accommodate the new additional attributes. However, by passing only the instance pointer, the interface does not have to change. Only the **StoreRecord** method would need to be changed to reflect the new attributes.

Note the importance of the interface to the method clients. In this example, when the driver program invokes **OpenCheckingAccount**, it does not know how the process is accomplished. When CheckingAccount subsequently invokes **StoreRecord** in CheckingDataManager, it is not concerned with how the information is stored. The manner in which the CheckingDataManager stores the instance is totally hidden from the clients: it is encapsulated. If at some later time we wanted to change the storage from an ISAM file to a relational database, we would simply change the appropriate CheckingDataManager methods; the implementation would be hidden from the clients of these methods, thus greatly simplifying system maintenance.

The second instance method added to CheckingAccount is **RetrieveCheckingAccount**. This method has been added to allow clients to retrieve information about existing accounts. The OID for this method is shown in Figure 7.9. At step 1, the driver program invokes **RetrieveCheckingAccount** in the CheckingAccount class. CheckingAccount then creates an instance of CheckingAccount

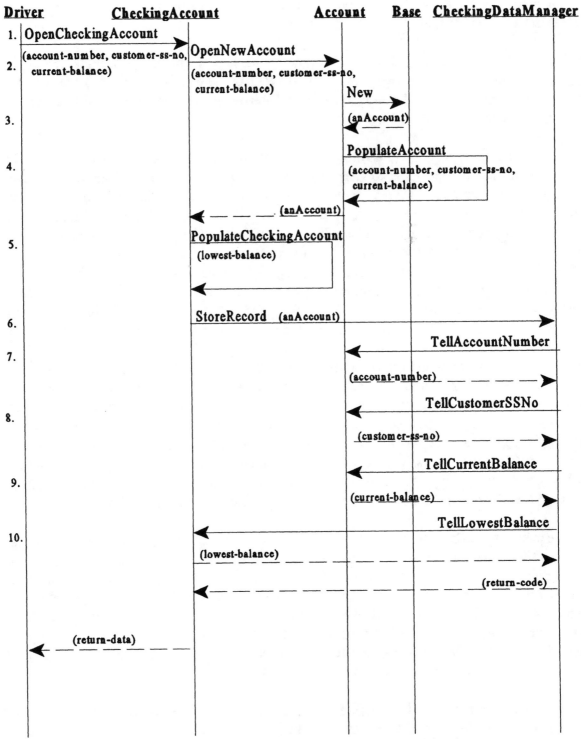

Figure 7.7   Object Interaction Diagram—OpenCheckingAccount

```
*-------------------------------------------------------------
*   StoreRecord is a DataManager instance method designed to
*    write a new ISAM record for a given account number
*-------------------------------------------------------

METHOD-ID. "StoreRecord".

LINKAGE SECTION.
01  anAccount    USAGE IS OBJECT REFERENCE.
01  return-code-ls              PIC X(3).


PROCEDURE DIVISION  USING       anAccount
                    RETURNING return-code-ls.


    INVOKE anAccount  "TellAccountNumber"
        RETURNING  account-number-ws
    END-INVOKE
    INVOKE anAccount  "TellCustomerSSNo"
        RETURNING  customer-ss-no-ws
    END-INVOKE
    INVOKE anAccount  "TellCurrentBalance"
        RETURNING  current-balance-ws
    END-INVOKE
    INVOKE anAccount  "TellLowestBalance"
        RETURNING  lowest-balance-ws
    END-INVOKE

    MOVE account-number-ws  TO account-number-fs
    MOVE customer-ss-no-ws  TO customer-ss-no-fs
    MOVE current-balance-ws TO current-balance-fs
    MOVE lowest-balance-ws  TO lowest-balance-fs

    OPEN I-O Checking-File
    WRITE Checking-Record
      INVALID KEY
         MOVE "DUP" to return-code-ls
      NOT INVALID KEY
         MOVE "OK" to return-code-ls
    END-WRITE
    CLOSE Checking-File

    EXIT METHOD.
END METHOD "StoreRecord".
```

Figure 7.8 StoreRecord Method

which in reality is a composite instance of Account and CheckingAccount (step 2). CheckingAccount next invokes **RetrieveRecord** in CheckingDataManager (step 3). In CheckingDataManager, the file is opened and read. If the account is found, **PopulateAccount** and **PopulateCheckingAccount** are invoked (steps 4 and 5).

Each of these methods populates the dynamic instances with the information retrieved from the file. Let's think about this for a second. We create the dynamic instance, find the account in the file, and then populate the dynamic instance with the information obtained from the file. Why? First, we obviously want to know if the record exists before we can do anything with it (for example, update the balance). Second, an Account instance must be created so that we can work with the instance in memory. Without the instance in memory, we would not have access to the methods and data associated with the instance and the instance's superclass. Remember, the data are protected by methods. So, the only way to get to the data is through methods. Thus, we must create a CheckingAccount instance to allow access to the methods (and data).

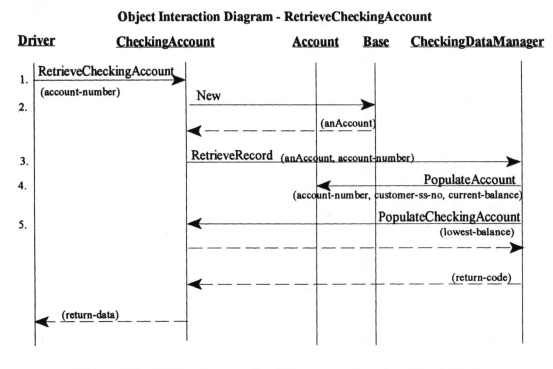

Figure 7.9 Object Interaction Diagram—RetrieveCheckingAccount

The CustomerDataManager Class

Thus far, we have demonstrated the creation of persistent CheckingAccount instances using the new data management class CheckingDataManager. However, we would not expect to have a CheckingAccount instance without an associated Customer. Therefore, let's add the capability needed to create persistent Customer instances.

We will create a second data management class called <u>CustomerDataManager</u>, which does essentially the same things as <u>CheckingDataManager</u>.   <u>CustomerDataManager</u> has the same method names with similar interfaces and performs functions similar to <u>CheckingDataManager</u>.

These programs are listed at the end of the chapter. For comparison, the OID for adding and retrieving a customer are shown in Figures 7.10 and 7.11, respectively. Note the overwhelming similarity with the same methods for adding and retrieving a CheckingAccount.

OBJECT PROGRAMMING AT ITS FINEST—EASY MAINTENANCE

In this chapter, we have demonstrated how to store instances in indexed sequential files. However, let's assume that we want to change to a relational database. To the client programs, the change is hidden. We will change the data management class methods to store the information in a relational database, yet we do not have to change the client programs. The interface stays the same, so the client never knows that the storage has changed. This is object programming at its finest—changes are localized and hidden. Maintenance becomes a much simpler task. Modifications are generally made in only one place. Again, unless the interface changes, clients never realize that a change has occurred.

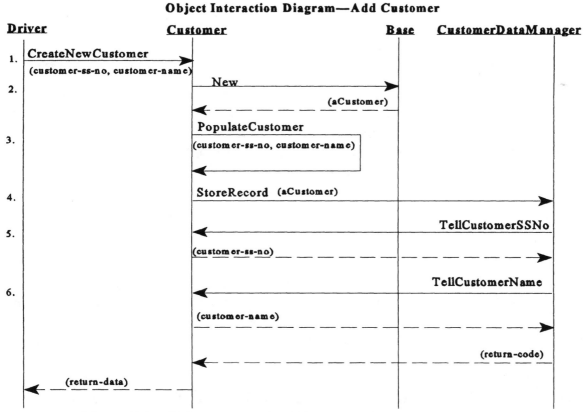

Figure 7.10 Object Interaction Diagram—CreateNewCustomer

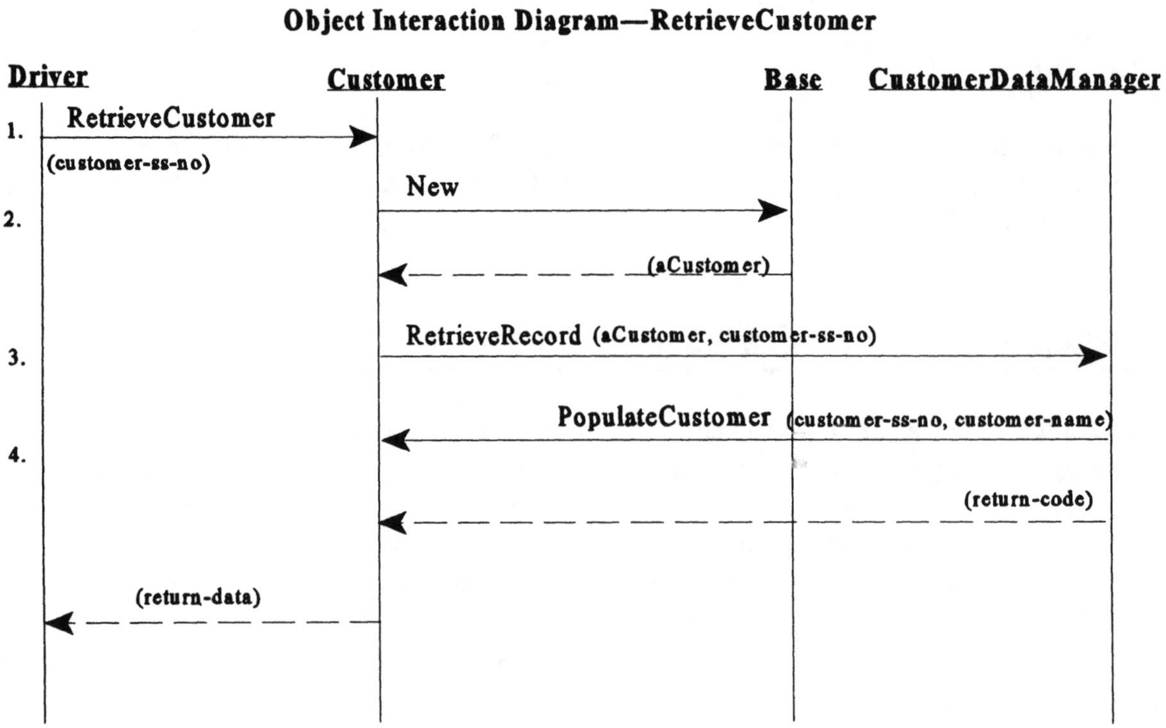

Object Interaction Diagram—RetrieveCustomer

Figure 7.11   Object Interaction Diagram—RetrieveCustomer

CLASS INTERFACES

We now have persistent instances that can be stored on disk and retrieved at a later time. The interfaces should now be set. Although we may add methods later, the current interfaces should not change. This ensures the stability of the system from the client's point of view. At the end of the chapter, all of the interface descriptions are listed in the Class Descriptions section. This information is very important as we begin to reuse class programs because we need to know the interface.

SUMMARY

This chapter has focused on the data management classes. Here we developed two classes to provide data management services: CheckingDataManager and CustomerDataManager. These classes provide services through simple, standardized method interfaces: **DeleteRecord**, **RetrieveRecord**, **StoreRecord**, and **UpdateRecord**. These methods and their interfaces completely hide the physical implementation of the data storage technique employed. This chapter also developed one new problem domain class, Customer.

You should now understand one technique for storing data in an OO system. The next chapter develops user interface classes, yet continues to use the class programs presented in this chapter **UNCHANGED!** This reuse of class programs illustrates one primary advantage of using OO development. We continue to expand the credit union system, yet modifications to the existing class programs are not required.

KEY TERMS

Dynamic instance
Persistent instance

REVIEW QUESTIONS

1. Do all business information systems require persistent data storage? Why or why not?

2. What are some methods to store persistent instances?

3. What are two broad approaches to mapping instances to files?

4. Although methods in the Account class were modified in this chapter, the method interface remained the same. Why is it desirable to avoid modifying the interface? What problems can result from modifying the interface?

5. If in the chapter example, a relational database was used instead of a flat file, what class programs would need to be modified? To what extent, if any, would the modifications affect the class interfaces?

6. In this chapter, CheckingAccount passes only the instance pointer anAccount to the **StoreRecord** method in CheckingDataManager. Explain why this was done instead of passing all of the attributes for a checking account instance.

EXERCISE

1. Create a new data management class program, SavingsDataManager, to provide persistent instances for the SavingsAccount class. Also, modify the SavingsAccount class program accordingly. (*Hint*: You will need to add some new methods and modify some existing methods.) Follow the example of the CheckingAccount class very carefully.

BIBLIOGRAPHY

Booch, G. <u>Object-Oriented Design with Applications</u>. Benjamin-Cummings, 1991.

Brown, D. <u>An Introduction to Object-Oriented Analysis</u>. John Wiley & Sons, 1997.

Firesmith, D. G. <u>Object-Oriented Requirements Analysis and Logical Design</u>. John Wiley & Sons, 1993.

Jacobson, I., et al. <u>Object-Oriented Software Engineering: A Use Case Driven Approach</u>. Addison-Wesley, 1992.

Rumbaugh, J., et al. <u>Object-Oriented Modeling and Design</u>. Prentice-Hall, 1991.

Taylor, D. A. <u>Object-Oriented Systems: Planning and Implementation</u>. John Wiley & Sons, 1992.

CLASS DESCRIPTIONS

1. **CH7-ACCT** is a class program for Account. It is a copy of CH6-ACCT with the addition of method TellAccountNumber.

   Attributes:
   ```
   account-number    PIC 9(5)
   customer-ss-no    PIC 9(5)
   current-balance   PIC S9(5)V99
   ```

   Factory Method:
   ```
   OpenNewAccount   USING account-number, customer-ss-no,
                    current-balance
                    RETURNING anAccount
   ```

   Instance Methods:
   ```
   ChangeCurrentBalance        USING current-balance
   <private> PopulateAccount USING account-number
      customer-ss-no,current-balance
   TellCurrentBalance          RETURNING current-balance
   #TellAccountNumber          RETURNING account-number
   TellCustomerSSNo            RETURNING customer-ss-no
   ```

   #New instance method for Chapter 7.

2. **CH7-CHEK** is a class program for CheckingAccount. It is a copy of CH6-CHEK with the additional instance methods: CloseCheckingAccount and RetrieveCheckingAccount.

   Attribute: `lowest-balance   PIC S9(5)V99`

   Factory Method:
   ```
   OpenCheckingAccount USING account-number, customer-ss-no
                       current-balance
                       RETURNING return-data
   ```

   *Instance Methods:
   ```
   #CloseCheckingAccount USING anAccount RETURNING return-
                         code
   ComputeServiceCharge    RETURNING service-charge
   <private> PopulateCheckingAccount USING lowest-balance
   RecordCheck             USING amount-of-check, anAccount
   RecordDeposit           USING amount-of-deposit, anAccount
   #RetrieveCheckingAccount  USING account-number
                           RETURNING return-data*
   TellLowestBalance       RETURNING lowest-balance
   ```

   # New instance method for Chapter 7 .

   * Return-data contains return-code and anAccount.

3. **CH7-CKDM** is a class program for CheckingDataManager.

 Attributes: none.

 Factory Methods:

```
DeleteRecord       USING anAccount RETURNING return-code
RetrieveRecord     USING anAccount, account-number
                   RETURNING return-code
StoreRecord        USING anAccount RETURNING return-code
UpdateRecord       USING anAccount RETURNING return-code
```

 Instance Methods: none

4. **CH7-CUST** is a class program for Customer.

 Attributes:

```
customer-ss-no     PIC 9(9)
customer-name      PIC X(20)
```

 Factory Methods:

```
CreateNewCustomer       USING customer-ss-no, customer-name
                        RETURNING return-data*
RetrieveCustomer        USING customer-ss-no RETURNING
                        return-data*
```

 Instance Methods:

```
<private> PopulateCustomer USING customer-ss-no,
                        customer-name
RemoveCustomer          USING aCustomer RETURNING return-data*
TellCustomerSSNo        RETURNING customer-ss-no
TellCustomerName        RETURNING customer-name
ChangeCustomerName      USING customer-name, aCustomer
                        RETURNING return-data*
```

 * Return-data contains return-code and aCustomer.

5. **CH7-CSDM** is a class program for CustomerDataManager.

 Attributes: none.

 Factory Methods:

```
DeleteRecord     USING aCustomer RETURNING return-code
RetrieveRecord   USING aCustomer, account-number
                 RETURNING return-code
StoreRecord      USING aCustomer RETURNING return-code
UpdateRecord     USING aCustomer RETURNING return-code
```

 Instance Methods: none

PROGRAM LISTINGS

Account Class

```
*   CH7-ACCT is a class program for Account.
*----------------------------------------------------------
```

```
 1    CLASS-ID. CH7-ACCT
 2         DATA IS PRIVATE
 3         INHERITS FROM Base.
 4
 5
 6    CLASS-CONTROL.
 7         Base        is class "Base"
 8         Account     is class "CH7-ACCT".
 9
10
11    CLASS-OBJECT.
12
13
14    *------ Factory Methods -------------------------------------
15    METHOD-ID. "OpenNewAccount".
16    LINKAGE SECTION.
17    01   anAccount    Usage is Object Reference.
18    01   account-number-ls            PIC 9(5).
19    01   customer-ss-no-ls            PIC 9(9).
20    01   current-balance-ls           PIC S9(5)V99.
21
22
23    PROCEDURE DIVISION
24         USING        account-number-ls
25                      customer-ss-no-ls
26                      current-balance-ls
27         RETURNING    anAccount.
28         INVOKE Self "New"
29             RETURNING anAccount
30         END-INVOKE
31
32
33         INVOKE anAccount "PopulateAccount"
34             USING account-number-ls
35                   customer-ss-no-ls
36                   current-balance-ls
37         END-INVOKE
38         EXIT METHOD.
39    END METHOD "OpenNewAccount".
40    END CLASS-OBJECT.
41
42
43    *-------Instance Methods ---------------------------------
44
45
46    OBJECT.
47    WORKING-STORAGE SECTION.
48    01   account-info-os.
49         05   account-number-os        PIC 9(5).
50         05   customer-ss-no-os        PIC 9(9).
51         05   current-balance-os       PIC S9(5)V99.
52    *----------------------------------------------------------
```

```
53
54          METHOD-ID.  "ChangeCurrentBalance".
55          LINKAGE SECTION.
56          01   current-balance-ls  Pic S9(5)V99.
57
58
59          PROCEDURE DIVISION  USING current-balance-ls.
60             MOVE current-balance-ls TO current-balance-os
61             EXIT METHOD.
62          END METHOD "ChangeCurrentBalance".
63          *------------------------------------------------------------
64
65
66          METHOD-ID.  "PopulateAccount".
67          LINKAGE SECTION.
68          01   account-number-ls           PIC 9(5).
69          01   customer-ss-no-ls           PIC 9(9).
70          01   current-balance-ls          PIC S9(5)V99.
71
72
73          PROCEDURE DIVISION USING       account-number-ls
74                                         customer-ss-no-ls
75                                         current-balance-ls.
76             MOVE account-number-ls  TO account-number-os
77             MOVE customer-ss-no-ls  TO customer-ss-no-os
78             MOVE current-balance-ls TO current-balance-os
79             EXIT METHOD.
80          END METHOD "PopulateAccount".
81          *------------------------------------------------------------
82          METHOD-ID.  "TellAccountNumber".
83          LINKAGE SECTION.
84          01   account-number-ls  Pic 9(5).
85          PROCEDURE DIVISION  RETURNING account-number-ls.
86             MOVE account-number-os TO account-number-ls
87             EXIT METHOD.
88          END METHOD "TellAccountNumber".
89          *------------------------------------------------------------
90
91
92          METHOD-ID.  "TellCurrentBalance".
93          LINKAGE SECTION.
94          01   current-balance-ls  Pic S9(5)V99.
95          PROCEDURE DIVISION  RETURNING current-balance-ls.
96             MOVE current-balance-os TO current-balance-ls
97             EXIT METHOD.
98          END METHOD "TellCurrentBalance".
99          *------------------------------------------------------------
100         METHOD-ID.  "TellCustomerSSNo".
101         LINKAGE SECTION.
102         01   customer-ss-no-ls          PIC 9(9).
103         PROCEDURE DIVISION  returning customer-ss-no-ls.
104            MOVE customer-ss-no-os TO customer-ss-no-ls
105            EXIT METHOD.
106         END METHOD "TellCustomerSSNo".
107         END OBJECT.
108
109         END CLASS CH7-ACCT.
```

CheckingAccount Class

```
*   CH7-CHEK is a class program for CheckingAccount which is a
*     subclass of CH7-ACCT, Account.  Used to demonstrate
*     persistent CheckingAccount objects stored in an ISAM file.
*-------------------------------------------------------------
 1    CLASS-ID.  CH7-CHEK
 2        DATA IS PRIVATE
 3        INHERITS FROM CH7-ACCT.
 4
 5    OBJECT SECTION.
 6    CLASS-CONTROL.
 7        Account              is class "CH7-ACCT"
 8        CheckingAccount      is class "CH7-CHEK"
 9        CheckingDataManager is class "CH7-CKDM".
10
11    CLASS-OBJECT.
12
13    *------ Factory Methods ------------------------------------
14
15
16    METHOD-ID. "OpenCheckingAccount".
17    WORKING-STORAGE SECTION.
18    01  lowest-balance-ws          PIC S9(5)V99.
19    LINKAGE SECTION.
20    01  account-number-ls          PIC 9(5).
21    01  customer-ss-no-ls          PIC 9(9).
22    01  current-balance-ls         PIC S9(5)V99.
23    01  return-data-ls.
24        05  return-code-ls         PIC X(3).
25        05  anAccount         USAGE IS OBJECT REFERENCE.
26
27
28    PROCEDURE DIVISION USING      account-number-ls
29                                  customer-ss-no-ls
30                                  current-balance-ls
31                    RETURNING return-data-ls.
32
33
34        INVOKE Self "OpenNewAccount"
35            USING        account-number-ls
36                         customer-ss-no-ls
37                         current-balance-ls
38            RETURNING    anAccount
39        END-INVOKE
40
41
42        MOVE current-balance-ls TO lowest-balance-ws
43        INVOKE anAccount "PopulateCheckingAccount"
44            USING  lowest-balance-ws
45        END-INVOKE
46
47
48    *   create a record for the checking account in the ISAM file
49        INVOKE CheckingDataManager "StoreRecord"
50            USING       anAccount
51            RETURNING   return-code-ls
52        END-INVOKE
```

```
53              EXIT METHOD.
54           END METHOD "OpenCheckingAccount".
55           *------------------------------------------------------
56
57           METHOD-ID. "RetrieveCheckingAccount".
58
59           WORKING-STORAGE SECTION.
60           01   return-code-ws                    PIC X(3).
61           01   anAccount-ws          USAGE IS OBJECT REFERENCE.
62           LINKAGE SECTION.
63           01   account-number-ls          PIC 9(5).
64
65
66           01   return-data-ls.
67              05   return-code-ls          PIC X(3).
68              05   anAccount-ls          USAGE IS OBJECT REFERENCE.
69
70
71           PROCEDURE DIVISION USING          account-number-ls
72                          RETURNING     return-data-ls.
73        *   create an instance of CheckingAccount
74              INVOKE Self "New"
75                 RETURNING anAccount-ws
76              END-INVOKE
77        *   retrieve the CheckingAccount data from the ISAM file
78              INVOKE CheckingDataManager "RetrieveRecord"
79                 USING          anAccount-ws
80                             account-number-ls
81                 RETURNING     return-code-ws
82              END-INVOKE
83              MOVE return-code-ws TO return-code-ls
84              SET  anAccount-ls   TO anAccount-ws
85              EXIT METHOD.
86           END METHOD "RetrieveCheckingAccount".
87           END CLASS-OBJECT.
88
89           *------Instance Methods -------------------------------
90
91           OBJECT.
92           OBJECT-STORAGE SECTION.
93           01   checking-account-attributes-os.
94              05   lowest-balance-os       PIC S9(5)V99.
95           *------------------------------------------------------
96           METHOD-ID. "CloseCheckingAccount".
97           WORKING-STORAGE SECTION.
98           01   return-code-ws             PIC X(3).
99           LINKAGE SECTION.
100          01   anAccount   USAGE IS OBJECT REFERENCE.
101
102
103          PROCEDURE DIVISION  USING anAccount.
104              INVOKE CheckingDataManager "DeleteRecord"
105                 USING          anAccount
106                 RETURNING     return-code-ws
107              END-INVOKE
108              EXIT METHOD.
```

```
109      END METHOD "CloseCheckingAccount".
110      *-----------------------------------------------------------
111      METHOD-ID. "ComputeServiceCharge".
112      LINKAGE SECTION.
113      01  service-charge-ls            Pic 9(4)V99.
114      PROCEDURE DIVISION RETURNING service-charge-ls.
115          IF lowest-balance-os < 100.00
116              MOVE 5.00 to service-charge-ls
117          ELSE
118              MOVE zeros to service-charge-ls
119          END-IF
120          EXIT METHOD.
121      END METHOD "ComputeServiceCharge".
122      *-----------------------------------------------------------
123      METHOD-ID. "PopulateCheckingAccount".
124      LINKAGE SECTION.
125      01  lowest-balance-ls         .PIC 9(5)V99.
126      PROCEDURE DIVISION USING lowest-balance-ls.
127          MOVE lowest-balance-ls TO lowest-balance-os
128          EXIT METHOD.
129      END METHOD "PopulateCheckingAccount".
130      *-----------------------------------------------------------
131      METHOD-ID. "RecordCheck".
132      WORKING-STORAGE SECTION.
133      01  current-balance-ws           PIC S9(5)V99.
134      01  return-code-ws               PIC X(3).
135      LINKAGE SECTION.
136      01  amount-of-check-ls           PIC 9(5)V99.
137      01  anAccount        USAGE IS OBJECT REFERENCE.
138
139
140      PROCEDURE DIVISION USING      amount-of-check-ls
141                                    anAccount.
142          INVOKE Self  "TellCurrentBalance"
143              RETURNING   current-balance-ws
144          END-INVOKE
145          SUBTRACT amount-of-check-ls FROM  current-balance-ws
146          INVOKE Self  "ChangeCurrentBalance"
147              USING  current-balance-ws
148          END-INVOKE
149          IF current-balance-ws <  lowest-balance-os
150              MOVE current-balance-ws TO lowest-balance-os
151          END-IF
152          INVOKE CheckingDataManager "UpdateRecord"
153              USING       anAccount
154              RETURNING   return-code-ws
155          END-INVOKE
156          EXIT METHOD.
157      END METHOD "RecordCheck".
158      *-----------------------------------------------------------
159      METHOD-ID. "RecordDeposit".
160      WORKING-STORAGE SECTION.
161      01  current-balance-ws           PIC S9(5)V99.
162      01  return-code-ws               PIC X(3).
163      LINKAGE SECTION.
164      01  amount-of-deposit-ls         PIC 9(5)V99.
165      01  anAccount        USAGE IS OBJECT REFERENCE.
166
167
```

```
168          PROCEDURE DIVISION USING amount-of-deposit-ls
169                                  anAccount.
170             INVOKE Self  "TellCurrentBalance"
171                 RETURNING  current-balance-ws
172             END-INVOKE
173             ADD amount-of-deposit-ls TO  current-balance-ws
174             INVOKE Self  "ChangeCurrentBalance"
175                 USING  current-balance-ws
176             END-INVOKE
177             INVOKE CheckingDataManager "UpdateRecord"
178                 USING       anAccount
179                 RETURNING   return-code-ws
180             END-INVOKE
181             EXIT METHOD.
182          END METHOD "RecordDeposit".
183          *-------------------------------------------------------------
184          METHOD-ID. "TellLowestBalance".
185          LINKAGE SECTION.
186          01  lowest-balance-ls          Pic S9(5)V99.
187          PROCEDURE DIVISION  RETURNING lowest-balance-ls.
188             MOVE lowest-balance-os to lowest-balance-ls
189             EXIT METHOD.
190          END METHOD "TellLowestBalance".
191          END OBJECT.
192
193
194          END CLASS CH7-CHEK.
```

CheckingDataManager Class

```
*   CH7-CKDM is a class program for DataManager which is a
*     class to manage data for Account & CheckingAccount to show
*     persistent objects stored in an ISAM file.
*------------------------------------------------------------
```

```
 1        CLASS-ID.   CH7-CKDM.
 2
 3        FILE-CONTROL.
 4            SELECT Checking-File ASSIGN TO "CH7-CHKG.DAT"
 5                ORGANIZATION IS INDEXED
 6                ACCESS IS RANDOM
 7                RECORD KEY IS account-number-fs.
 8
 9
10        OBJECT SECTION.
11        CLASS-CONTROL.
12            Account             is class "CH7-ACCT"
13            CheckingAccount     is class "CH7-CHEK"
14            CheckingDataManager is class "CH7-CKDM".
15
16
17        FILE SECTION.
18        FD  Checking-File.
19        01  Checking-Record.
20            05   account-number-fs       PIC 9(5).
21            05   customer-ss-no-fs       PIC 9(9).
22            05   current-balance-fs      PIC S9(5)v99.
23            05   lowest-balance-fs       PIC S9(5)v99.
24
25
26        WORKING-STORAGE SECTION.
27        01   account-number-ws           PIC 9(5).
28        01   customer-ss-no-ws           PIC 9(9).
29        01   current-balance-ws          PIC S9(5)V99.
30        01   lowest-balance-ws           PIC S9(5)V99.
31
32
33        CLASS-OBJECT.
34
35
36        *------ Factory Methods -------------------------------------
37
38
39        *---------------------------------------------------------
40        *   DeleteRecord is a DataManager method designed to
41        *     Delete an ISAM record for a given account
42        *---------------------------------------------------------
43
44
45        METHOD-ID. "DeleteRecord".
46
47
48        LINKAGE SECTION.
49        01   anAccount  USAGE IS OBJECT REFERENCE.
50        01   return-code-ls               PIC X(3).
51
52
```

```
53         PROCEDURE DIVISION USING       anAccount
54                          RETURNING return-code-ls.
55             INVOKE anAccount   "TellAccountNumber"
56                 RETURNING   account-number-ws
57             END-INVOKE
58     *  we must first read the record before doing the delete
59             MOVE account-number-ws to account-number-fs
60             OPEN I-O Checking-File
61             READ Checking-File
62                INVALID KEY
63                    MOVE "NRF" to return-code-ls
64                NOT INVALID KEY
65                    DELETE Checking-File
66                        INVALID KEY
67                            MOVE "BAD" to return-code-ls
68                        NOT INVALID KEY
69                            MOVE "OK" to return-code-ls
70                    END-DELETE
71             END-READ
72             CLOSE Checking-File
73             EXIT METHOD.
74         END METHOD "DeleteRecord".
75          *-----------------------------------------------------
76          *  RetrieveRecord is a DataManager method designed to
77          *   Retrieve an ISAM record for a given account number
78          *   and to populate the account instance provided
79          *-----------------------------------------------------
80
81
82          METHOD-ID. "RetrieveRecord".
83
84
85          LINKAGE SECTION.
86          01  anAccount         Usage is Object Reference.
87          01  account-number-ls                PIC 9(5).
88          01  return-code-ls                   PIC X(3).
89
90
91          PROCEDURE DIVISION USING        anAccount
92                                          account-number-ls
93                          RETURNING      return-code-ls.
94
95
96          *  retrieve the CheckingAccount data from the ISAM file
97              MOVE account-number-ls TO account-number-fs
98              OPEN I-O Checking-File
99              READ Checking-File
100                 INVALID KEY
101                     MOVE "NRF" to return-code-ls
102                 NOT INVALID KEY
103                     MOVE "OK" to return-code-ls
104                     INVOKE anAccount "PopulateCheckingAccount"
105                         USING lowest-balance-fs
106                     END-INVOKE
107                     INVOKE anAccount "PopulateAccount"
108                         USING   account-number-fs   customer-ss-no-fs
109                                    current-balance-fs
110                     END-INVOKE
111              END-READ
112              CLOSE Checking-File
```

```
113          EXIT METHOD.
114       END METHOD "RetrieveRecord".
115        *-----------------------------------------------------
116        *  StoreRecord is a DataManager instance method designed to
117        *    write a new ISAM record for a given account number
118        *-----------------------------------------------------
119
120
121        METHOD-ID. "StoreRecord".
122
123
124        LINKAGE SECTION.
125        01   anAccount    USAGE IS OBJECT REFERENCE.
126        01   return-code-ls              PIC X(3).
127
128
129        PROCEDURE DIVISION  USING      anAccount
130                            RETURNING return-code-ls.
131
132
133           INVOKE anAccount   "TellAccountNumber"
134              RETURNING  account-number-ws
135           END-INVOKE
136           INVOKE anAccount   "TellCustomerSSNo"
137              RETURNING  customer-ss-no-ws
138           END-INVOKE
139           INVOKE anAccount   "TellCurrentBalance"
140              RETURNING  current-balance-ws
141           END-INVOKE
142           INVOKE anAccount   "TellLowestBalance"
143              RETURNING  lowest-balance-ws
144           END-INVOKE
145
146
147           MOVE account-number-ws   TO account-number-fs
148           MOVE customer-ss-no-ws   TO customer-ss-no-fs
149           MOVE current-balance-ws TO current-balance-fs
150           MOVE lowest-balance-ws   TO lowest-balance-fs
151
152
153           OPEN I-O Checking-File
154           WRITE Checking-Record
155             INVALID KEY
156                MOVE "DUP" to return-code-ls
157             NOT INVALID KEY
158                MOVE "OK" to return-code-ls
159           END-WRITE
160           CLOSE Checking-File
161
162
163           EXIT METHOD.
164       END METHOD "StoreRecord".
165        *-----------------------------------------------------
166        *  UpdateRecord is a DataManager method designed to
167        *    Read, update & Rewrite the updated ISAM record for a
168        *    given account
169        *-----------------------------------------------------
170
171
172        METHOD-ID. "UpdateRecord".
```

```
173
174            LINKAGE SECTION.
175            01   anAccount        USAGE IS OBJECT REFERENCE.
176            01   return-code-ls               PIC X(3).
177
178
179            PROCEDURE DIVISION USING       anAccount
180                               RETURNING return-code-ls.
181
182
183                INVOKE anAccount   "TellAccountNumber"
184                    RETURNING   account-number-ws
185                END-INVOKE
186                INVOKE anAccount   "TellCustomerSSNo"
187                    RETURNING   customer-ss-no-ws
188                END-INVOKE
189                INVOKE anAccount   "TellCurrentBalance"
190                    RETURNING   current-balance-ws
191                END-INVOKE
192                INVOKE anAccount   "TellLowestBalance"
193                    RETURNING   lowest-balance-ws
194                END-INVOKE
195
196
197        *    retrieve & update the CheckingAccount data from the ISAM file
198                MOVE account-number-ws to account-number-fs
199                OPEN I-O Checking-File
200                READ Checking-File
201                    INVALID KEY
202                        MOVE "NRF" to return-code-ls
203                    NOT INVALID KEY
204                        MOVE customer-ss-no-ws   TO customer-ss-no-fs
205                        MOVE current-balance-ws TO current-balance-fs
206                        MOVE lowest-balance-ws   TO lowest-balance-fs
207                        REWRITE Checking-Record
208                            INVALID KEY
209                                MOVE "BAD" to return-code-ls
210                            NOT INVALID KEY
211                                MOVE "OK" to return-code-ls
212                        END-REWRITE
213                END-READ
214                CLOSE Checking-File
215                EXIT METHOD.
216            END METHOD "UpdateRecord".
217            END CLASS-OBJECT.
218            *------Instance Methods -------------------------------------
219
220
221            OBJECT.
222            OBJECT-STORAGE SECTION.
223            END OBJECT.
224
225
226            END CLASS CH7-CKDM.
227
228
```

Customer Class

```
        *  CH7-CUST is a class program for Customer.
        *-----------------------------------------------------------
 1        CLASS-ID.  CH7-CUST
 2            DATA IS PRIVATE
 3            INHERITS FROM Base.
 4
 5
 6        OBJECT SECTION.
 7        CLASS-CONTROL.
 8            Base                is class "Base"
 9            Customer            is class "CH7-CUST"
10            CustomerDataManager is class "CH7-CSDM".
11
12
13        CLASS-OBJECT.
14
15
16        *------ Factory Methods -----------------------------------
17
18
19        *----------------------------------------------------------
20        *  CreateNewCustomer is a factory method for Customer to:
21        *    1. Create a Customer instance
22        *    2. Invoke PopulateCustomer to populate the instance
23        *    3. Invoke StoreRecord in  CustomerDataManager class to
24        *       Create an ISAM record for the instance
25        *----------------------------------------------------------
26        METHOD-ID.  "CreateNewCustomer".
27
28
29        LINKAGE SECTION.
30        01  customer-ss-no-ls          PIC 9(9).
31        01  customer-name-ls           PIC X(20).
32        01  return-data-ls.
33            05  return-code-ls         PIC X(3).
34            05  aCustomer        USAGE IS OBJECT REFERENCE.
35
36
37        PROCEDURE DIVISION USING      customer-ss-no-ls
38                                      customer-name-ls
39                     RETURNING return-data-ls.
40
41
42            INVOKE Self "New"
43                RETURNING aCustomer
44            END-INVOKE
45
46
47            INVOKE aCustomer "PopulateCustomer"
48                USING customer-ss-no-ls
49                      customer-name-ls
50            END-INVOKE
51
52
53        *  create a record for the checking account in the ISAM file
54            INVOKE CustomerDataManager "StoreRecord"
```

```
55                USING        aCustomer
56                RETURNING    return-code-ls
57            END-INVOKE
58            EXIT METHOD.
59         END METHOD "CreateNewCustomer".
60         *-------------------------------------------------------
61         *   RetrieveCustomer is a factory method for Customer to:
62         *     1.Create a Customer instance
63         *     2.Retrieve the ISAM record for a particular Customer
64         *-------------------------------------------------------
65
66
67         METHOD-ID. "RetrieveCustomer".
68
69
70         WORKING-STORAGE SECTION.
71         01   return-code-ws              PIC X(3).
72         01   aCustomer-ws     USAGE IS OBJECT REFERENCE.
73
74
75         LINKAGE SECTION.
76         01   customer-ss-no-ls           PIC 9(5).
77         01   return-data-ls.
78            05   return-code-ls        PIC X(3).
79            05   aCustomer-ls     USAGE IS OBJECT REFERENCE.
80
81
82         PROCEDURE DIVISION USING        customer-ss-no-ls
83                           RETURNING    return-data-ls.
84
85
86         *   create an instance of CheckingAccount
87            INVOKE Self "New"
88                RETURNING aCustomer-ws
89            END-INVOKE
90
91
92         *   retrieve the Customer data from the ISAM file
93            INVOKE CustomerDataManager "RetrieveRecord"
94                USING        aCustomer-ws
95                             customer-ss-no-ls
96                RETURNING    return-code-ws
97            END-INVOKE
98            MOVE return-code-ws TO return-code-ls
99            SET  aCustomer-ls   TO aCustomer-ws
100           EXIT METHOD.
101        END METHOD "RetrieveCustomer".
102        END CLASS-OBJECT.
103
104
105        *------Instance Methods -------------------------------------
106
107
108        OBJECT.
109        OBJECT-STORAGE SECTION.
110        01   customer-attributes-os.
111           05   customer-ss-no-os       PIC 9(9).
112           05   customer-name-os        PIC X(20).
113        *-------------------------------------------------------
114
```

```
115        METHOD-ID.  "PopulateCustomer".
116
117
118        LINKAGE SECTION.
119        * Customer Attributes
120        01   customer-ss-no-ls        PIC 9(9).
121        01   customer-name-ls         PIC X(20).
122
123
124        PROCEDURE DIVISION USING customer-ss-no-ls
125                                 customer-name-ls.
126            MOVE customer-ss-no-ls TO customer-ss-no-os
127            MOVE customer-name-ls  TO customer-name-os
128            EXIT METHOD.
129        END METHOD "PopulateCustomer".
130        *-----------------------------------------------------
131        *   RemoveCustomer is an Instance method for Customer
132        *      designed to INVOKE DeleteRecord in CustomerDataManager to
133        *      remove an existing Customer record from the ISAM file.
134        *-----------------------------------------------------
135        METHOD-ID.  "RemoveCustomer".
136
137
138        WORKING-STORAGE SECTION.
139        01   return-code-ws              PIC X(3).
140        LINKAGE SECTION.
141        01   aCustomer    USAGE IS OBJECT REFERENCE.
142        01   return-data-ls.
143            05   return-code-ls          PIC X(3).
144            05   aCustomer-return-ls   USAGE IS OBJECT REFERENCE.
145        PROCEDURE DIVISION  USING       aCustomer
146                           RETURNING   return-data-ls.
147
148
149            INVOKE CustomerDataManager "DeleteRecord"
150                USING       aCustomer
151                RETURNING   return-code-ws
152            END-INVOKE
153            MOVE return-code-ws TO return-code-ls
154            EXIT METHOD.
155        END METHOD "RemoveCustomer".
156        *-----------------------------------------------------
157        METHOD-ID.  "TellCustomerSSNo".
158
159
160        LINKAGE SECTION.
161        * Customer Attributes
162        01   customer-ss-no-ls        PIC 9(9).
163
164
165        PROCEDURE DIVISION RETURNING customer-ss-no-ls.
166            MOVE customer-ss-no-os TO customer-ss-no-ls
167            EXIT METHOD.
168        END METHOD "TellCustomerSSNo".
169        *-----------------------------------------------------
170        METHOD-ID.  "TellCustomerName".
171
172
173        LINKAGE SECTION.
174        * Customer Attributes
```

```
175          01   customer-name-ls        PIC X(20).
176
177
178       PROCEDURE DIVISION RETURNING customer-name-ls.
179          MOVE customer-name-os TO customer-name-ls
180          EXIT METHOD.
181       END METHOD "TellCustomerName".
182
183
184
185
186       *-----------------------------------------------------
187       METHOD-ID. "ChangeCustomerName".
188
189
190       WORKING-STORAGE SECTION.
191       01   return-code-ws           PIC X(3).
192
193
194       LINKAGE SECTION.
195       01   customer-name-ls           PIC X(20).
196       01   aCustomer-ls    USAGE IS OBJECT REFERENCE.
197       01   RETURN-DATA-LS.
198          05   aCustomer-return-ls    USAGE IS OBJECT REFERENCE.
199          05   return-code-ls            PIC X(3).
200
201
202
203       PROCEDURE DIVISION USING customer-name-ls
204                               aCustomer-ls
205                         RETURNING return-data-ls.
206          MOVE customer-name-ls TO customer-name-os
207          INVOKE CustomerDataManager "UpdateRecord"
208             USING        aCustomer-ls
209             RETURNING    return-code-ws
210          END-INVOKE
211          MOVE return-code-ws      TO return-code-ls
212          SET aCustomer-return-ls TO aCustomer-ls
213          EXIT METHOD.
214       END METHOD "ChangeCustomerName".
215       END OBJECT.
216       END CLASS CH7-CUST.
```

CustomerDataManager Class

```
       *   CH7-CSDM is a class program for CustomerDataManager which is a
       *    class to manage data for Customer to show
       *    persistent objects stored in an ISAM file.
       *-------------------------------------------------------------

 1         CLASS-ID.  CH7-CSDM.
 2
 3
 4         FILE-CONTROL.
 5             SELECT Customer-File ASSIGN TO "CH7-CUST.DAT"
 6                 ORGANIZATION IS INDEXED
 7                 ACCESS IS RANDOM
 8                 RECORD KEY IS customer-ss-no-fs.
 9
10
11         OBJECT SECTION.
12         CLASS-CONTROL.
13             Customer             is class "CH7-CUST"
14             CustomerDataManager is class "CH7-CSDM".
15
16
17         FILE SECTION.
18         FD  Customer-File.
19         01  Customer-Record.
20             05   customer-ss-no-fs      PIC 9(9).
21             05   customer-name-fs       PIC X(20).
22
23
24         WORKING-STORAGE SECTION.
25         01  customer-ss-no-ws           PIC 9(9).
26         01  customer-name-ws            PIC X(20).
27
28
29         CLASS-OBJECT.
30
31
32         *------ Factory Methods ------------------------------------
33
34
35         *-------------------------------------------------------
36         *   DeleteRecord is a CustomerDataManager method designed to
37         *    Delete an ISAM record for a given customer
38         *-------------------------------------------------------
39
40
41         METHOD-ID. "DeleteRecord".
42
43
44         LINKAGE SECTION.
45         01  aCustomer  USAGE IS OBJECT REFERENCE.
46         01  return-code-ls             PIC X(3).
47
```

```
48          PROCEDURE DIVISION USING      aCustomer
49                          RETURNING return-code-ls.
50
51
52              INVOKE aCustomer  "TellCustomerSSNo"
53                 RETURNING  customer-ss-no-ws
54              END-INVOKE
55       *  we must first read the record before doing the delete
56              MOVE customer-ss-no-ws to customer-ss-no-fs
57              OPEN I-O Customer-File
58              READ Customer-File
59                  INVALID KEY
60                      MOVE "NRF" to return-code-ls
61                  NOT INVALID KEY
62                      DELETE Customer-File
63                          INVALID KEY
64                              MOVE "BAD" to return-code-ls
65                          NOT INVALID KEY
66                              MOVE "OK" to return-code-ls
67                      END-DELETE
68              END-READ
69              CLOSE Customer-File
70              EXIT METHOD.
71       END METHOD "DeleteRecord".
72       *------------------------------------------------------------
73       *  RetrieveRecord is a CustomerDataManager method designed to
74       *   Retrieve an ISAM record for a given customer
75       *   and to populate the account instance provided
76       *------------------------------------------------------------
77
78
79       METHOD-ID. "RetrieveRecord".
80
81
82       LINKAGE SECTION.
83       01   aCustomer       Usage is Object Reference.
84       01   customer-ss-no-ls                PIC 9(9).
85       01   return-code-ls                   PIC X(3).
86
87
88       PROCEDURE DIVISION USING      aCustomer
89                                     customer-ss-no-ls
90                          RETURNING   return-code-ls.
91
92
93       *  retrieve the Customer data from the ISAM file
94              MOVE customer-ss-no-ls to customer-ss-no-fs
95              OPEN I-O Customer-File
96              READ Customer-File
97                INVALID KEY
98                   MOVE "NRF" to return-code-ls
99                NOT INVALID KEY
100                  MOVE "OK" to return-code-ls
101             END-READ
102             CLOSE Customer-File
```

```
103
104    *  populate the Customer Instance
105        MOVE customer-ss-no-fs TO customer-ss-no-ws
106        MOVE customer-name-fs  TO customer-name-ws
107        INVOKE aCustomer "PopulateCustomer"
108            USING customer-ss-no-ws
109                  customer-name-ws
110        END-INVOKE
111        EXIT METHOD.
112     END METHOD "RetrieveRecord".
113     *-----------------------------------------------------
114    *  StoreRecord is a CustomerDataManager instance method
115    *    designed to Write a new ISAM record for a given customer
116     *-----------------------------------------------------
117
118
119     METHOD-ID. "StoreRecord".
120
121
122     LINKAGE SECTION.
123     01   aCustomer   USAGE IS OBJECT REFERENCE.
124     01   return-code-ls           PIC X(3).
125
126
127     PROCEDURE DIVISION  USING      aCustomer
128                        RETURNING return-code-ls.
129
130
131        INVOKE aCustomer "TellCustomerSSNo"
132            RETURNING   customer-ss-no-ws
133        END-INVOKE
134        INVOKE aCustomer "TellCustomerName"
135            RETURNING   customer-name-ws
136        END-INVOKE
137
138
139        MOVE customer-ss-no-ws  TO customer-ss-no-fs
140        MOVE customer-name-ws   TO customer-name-fs
141
142
143        OPEN I-O Customer-File
144        WRITE Customer-Record
145          INVALID KEY
146             MOVE "DUP" to return-code-ls
147          NOT INVALID KEY
148             MOVE "OK" to return-code-ls
149        END-WRITE
150        CLOSE Customer-File
151
152
153        EXIT METHOD.
154     END METHOD "StoreRecord".
155     *-----------------------------------------------------
156    *  UpdateRecord is a CustomerDataManager method designed to
157    *    Read, update & Rewrite the updated ISAM record for a
```

```
158          *    given customer
159          *----------------------------------------------------
160
161
162           METHOD-ID. "UpdateRecord".
163           LINKAGE SECTION.
164           01  aCustomer       USAGE IS OBJECT REFERENCE.
165           01  return-code-ls              PIC X(3).
166
167
168           PROCEDURE DIVISION USING      aCustomer
169                              RETURNING return-code-ls.
170              INVOKE aCustomer  "TellCustomerSSNo"
171                 RETURNING   customer-ss-no-ws
172              END-INVOKE
173              INVOKE aCustomer  "TellCustomerName"
174                 RETURNING   customer-name-ws
175              END-INVOKE
176          *   retrieve & update the customer data from the ISAM file
177              MOVE customer-ss-no-ws to customer-ss-no-fs
178              OPEN I-O Customer-File
179              READ Customer-File
180                 INVALID KEY
181                    MOVE "NRF" to return-code-ls
182                 NOT INVALID KEY
183                    MOVE "OK" to return-code-ls
184                    MOVE customer-ss-no-ws TO customer-ss-no-fs
185                    MOVE customer-name-ws  TO customer-name-fs
186                    REWRITE Customer-Record
187                       INVALID KEY
188                          MOVE "BAD" to return-code-ls
189                       NOT INVALID KEY
190                          MOVE "OK" to return-code-ls
191                    END-REWRITE
192              END-READ
193              CLOSE Customer-File
194              EXIT METHOD.
195           END METHOD "UpdateRecord".
196           END CLASS-OBJECT.
197          *------Instance Methods ------------------------------------
198
199
200           OBJECT.
201           OBJECT-STORAGE SECTION.
202           END OBJECT.
203
204
205           END CLASS CH7-CSDM.
206
207
```

Driver Program #1

```
*   CH7-PRG1 is a procedural program designed to INVOKE
*    various methods in Account and CheckingAccount classes
*    to illustrate the storage and retrieval of instance
*    data in an ISAM file.
*-------------------------------------------------------------
```

```
1      PROGRAM-ID. CH7-PRG1.
2
3
4      CLASS-CONTROL.
5        Account           IS CLASS "CH7-ACCT"
6        CheckingAccount IS CLASS "CH7-CHEK".
7
8
9      WORKING-STORAGE SECTION.
10
11
12     01   anything                    PIC X(1).
13     01   anAccount    USAGE IS OBJECT REFERENCE.
14
15
16     01   return-data-ws.
17        05   return-code-ws            PIC X(3).
18           88   no-record-found    VALUE "NRF".
19           88   duplicate-number   VALUE "DUP".
20           88   other-problem      VALUE "BAD".
21           88   account-found      VALUE "OK".
22        05   anAccount-ws     USAGE IS OBJECT REFERENCE.
23
24
25     01   amount-of-check-ws      PIC 9(5)v99.
26     01   amount-of-deposit-ws    PIC 9(5)v99.
27     01   service-charge-ws       Pic 9(4)V99.
28
29
30     *  Account Attributes
31
32
33     01   account-number-ws       PIC 9(5).
34     01   customer-ss-no-ws       PIC 9(9).
35     01   current-balance-ws      PIC S9(5)V99.
36
37
38     *  CheckingAccount Attributes
39
40
41     01   lowest-balance-ws       PIC S9(5)V99.
42
43
44     01   option                  PIC 9(1).
45     01   quit-flag               PIC X(1)  VALUE "N".
```

```
46                88   quit                                         VALUE "Y".
47
48
49          PROCEDURE DIVISION.
50
51
52              PERFORM UNTIL QUIT
53
54
55                  DISPLAY "    1. Open a New Checking Account"
56                  DISPLAY "    2. View Checking Account Information"
57                  DISPLAY "    3. Record a Check"
58                  DISPLAY "    4. Record a Deposit"
59                  DISPLAY "    5. Compute Service Charge"
60                  DISPLAY "    6. Close a Checking Account"
61                  DISPLAY "    9. Exit"
62                  DISPLAY "Enter option: " WITH NO ADVANCING
63                  ACCEPT option
64                  EVALUATE option
65                      WHEN 1
66                          PERFORM OPEN-ACCOUNT
67                      WHEN 2
68                          PERFORM DISPLAY-ACCOUNT-INFO
69                      WHEN 3
70                          PERFORM RECORD-CHECK
71                      WHEN 4
72                          PERFORM RECORD-DEPOSIT
73                      WHEN 5
74                          PERFORM COMPUTE-SERVICE-CHARGE
75                      WHEN 6
76                          PERFORM CLOSE-CHECKING-ACCOUNT
77                      WHEN 9
78                          SET QUIT TO TRUE
79                  END-EVALUATE
80              END-PERFORM
81              STOP RUN.
82
83
84          OPEN-ACCOUNT.
85              DISPLAY "enter account number for the new account:"
86                  WITH NO ADVANCING
87              ACCEPT account-number-ws
88              display "enter Customer SS number:" with no advancing
89              accept customer-ss-no-ws
90              DISPLAY "enter the current balance"
91                  WITH NO ADVANCING
92              ACCEPT current-balance-ws
93              INVOKE CheckingAccount "OpenCheckingAccount"
94                  USING      account-number-ws
95                             customer-ss-no-ws
96                             current-balance-ws
97                  RETURNING return-data-ws
98              END-INVOKE
99              IF duplicate-number
100                 PERFORM DISPLAY-DUP-NUMBER-MESSAGE
```

```
101         ELSE
102            IF other-problem
103                PERFORM DISPLAY-OTHER-PROBLEM-MESSAGE
104         END-IF.
105
106
107     DISPLAY-ACCOUNT-INFO.
108         display "enter account number:" with no advancing
109         accept account-number-ws
110         INVOKE CheckingAccount "RetrieveCheckingAccount"
111             USING       account-number-ws
112             RETURNING   return-data-ws
113         END-INVOKE
114
115
116         set anAccount to anAccount-ws
117
118
119         IF account-found
120             INVOKE anAccount "TellCustomerSSNo"
121                 RETURNING customer-ss-no-ws
122             END-INVOKE
123             DISPLAY "The Customer SS no is: ", customer-ss-no-ws
124
125
126             INVOKE anAccount "TellCurrentBalance"
127                 RETURNING current-balance-ws
128             END-INVOKE
129             DISPLAY "The Current Balance is: ", current-balance-ws
130             INVOKE anAccount "TellLowestBalance"
131                 RETURNING lowest-balance-ws
132             END-INVOKE
133             DISPLAY "The Lowest Balance is: ", lowest-balance-ws
134         else
135            IF no-record-found
136                PERFORM DISPLAY-NO-ACCT-FOUND-MESSAGE
137            ELSE
138                PERFORM DISPLAY-OTHER-PROBLEM-MESSAGE
139            END-IF
140         END-IF.
141
142
143     RECORD-CHECK.
144         display "enter account number:" with no advancing
145         accept account-number-ws
146         INVOKE CheckingAccount "RetrieveCheckingAccount"
147             USING       account-number-ws
148             RETURNING   return-data-ws
149         END-INVOKE
150
151
152         IF account-found
153             display "enter amount of check:" with no advancing
154             accept amount-of-check-ws
155             set anAccount to anAccount-ws
```

```
156              INVOKE anAccount "RecordCheck"
157                  USING    amount-of-check-ws
158                           anAccount
159              END-INVOKE
160              INVOKE anAccount "TellCurrentBalance"
161                  RETURNING current-balance-ws
162              END-INVOKE
163              DISPLAY "The Current Balance is: ", current-balance-ws
164              INVOKE anAccount "TellLowestBalance"
165                  RETURNING lowest-balance-ws
166              END-INVOKE
167              DISPLAY "The Lowest Balance is: ", lowest-balance-ws
168          ELSE
169              IF  no-record-found
170                  PERFORM DISPLAY-NO-ACCT-FOUND-MESSAGE
171              ELSE
172                  PERFORM DISPLAY-OTHER-PROBLEM-MESSAGE
173              END-IF
174          END-IF.
175
176
177      RECORD-DEPOSIT.
178          display "enter account number:" with no advancing
179          accept account-number-ws
180          INVOKE CheckingAccount "RetrieveCheckingAccount"
181              USING     account-number-ws
182              RETURNING  return-data-ws
183          END-INVOKE
184
185
186          IF account-found
187              display "enter amount of deposit:" with no advancing
188              accept amount-of-deposit-ws
189              set anAccount to anAccount-ws
190              INVOKE anAccount "RecordDeposit"
191                  USING    amount-of-deposit-ws
192                           anAccount
193              END-INVOKE
194                INVOKE anAccount "TellCurrentBalance"
195                    RETURNING current-balance-ws
196              END-INVOKE
197              DISPLAY "The Current Balance is: ", current-balance-ws
198              INVOKE anAccount "TellLowestBalance"
199                  RETURNING lowest-balance-ws
200              END-INVOKE
201              DISPLAY "The Lowest Balance is: ", lowest-balance-ws
202          ELSE
203              IF  no-record-found
204                  PERFORM DISPLAY-NO-ACCT-FOUND-MESSAGE
205              ELSE
206                  PERFORM DISPLAY-OTHER-PROBLEM-MESSAGE
207              END-IF
208          END-IF.
209
210
```

```
211    COMPUTE-SERVICE-CHARGE.
212        display "enter account number:" with no advancing
213        accept account-number-ws
214        INVOKE CheckingAccount "RetrieveCheckingAccount"
215            USING      account-number-ws
216            RETURNING  return-data-ws
217        END-INVOKE
218
219
220        IF account-found
221            INVOKE anAccount-ws "ComputeServiceCharge"
222                RETURNING   service-charge-ws
223            END-INVOKE
224            DISPLAY "Service Charge Amount is: ", service-charge-ws
225        ELSE
226            IF  no-record-found
227                PERFORM DISPLAY-NO-acct-FOUND-MESSAGE
228            ELSE
229                PERFORM DISPLAY-OTHER-PROBLEM-MESSAGE
230            END-IF
231        END-IF.
232
233
234    CLOSE-CHECKING-ACCOUNT.
235        display "enter account number:" with no advancing
236        accept account-number-ws
237        INVOKE CheckingAccount "RetrieveCheckingAccount"
238            USING      account-number-ws
239            RETURNING  return-data-ws
240        END-INVOKE
241        IF account-found
242            SET anAccount to anAccount-ws
243            INVOKE anAccount "CloseCheckingAccount"
244                USING anAccount
245            END-INVOKE
246        ELSE
247            IF  no-record-found
248                PERFORM DISPLAY-NO-ACCT-FOUND-MESSAGE
249            ELSE
250                PERFORM DISPLAY-OTHER-PROBLEM-MESSAGE
251            END-IF
252        END-IF.
253
254
255    DISPLAY-DUP-NUMBER-MESSAGE.
256        DISPLAY "This account number already exists"
257        Display "Press Any Key to Continue..."
258        Accept anything.
259
260
261    DISPLAY-NO-ACCT-FOUND-MESSAGE.
262        DISPLAY "This account cannot be found"
263        Display "Press Any Key to Continue..."
264        Accept anything.
265
```

```
266        DISPLAY-OTHER-PROBLEM-MESSAGE.
267            DISPLAY "Unknown Problem with ISAM file.."
268            Display "Press Any Key to Continue..."
269            Accept anything.
```

Driver Program #2

```
*  CH7-PRG2 is a procedural program designed to INVOKE
*  various methods in the Customer class
*  to illustrate the storage and retrieval of instance
*  data in an ISAM file.
*-----------------------------------------------------------
```

```
 1      PROGRAM-ID. CH7-PRG2.
 2
 3
 4      CLASS-CONTROL.
 5         Customer         IS CLASS "CH7-CUST".
 6
 7
 8      WORKING-STORAGE SECTION.
 9
10
11      01   anything                      PIC X(1).
12      01   aCustomer   USAGE IS OBJECT REFERENCE.
13
14
15      01   return-data-ws.
16           05   return-code-ws           PIC X(3).
17                88   no-record-found      VALUE "NRF".
18                88   duplicate-number     VALUE "DUP".
19                88   other-problem        VALUE "BAD".
20                88   customer-found       VALUE "OK".
21           05   aCustomer-ws     USAGE IS OBJECT REFERENCE.
22
23
24      *  Customer Attributes
25        01   customer-ss-no-ws         PIC 9(9).
26        01   customer-name-ws          PIC X(20).
27
28
29      01   option                        PIC 9(1).
30      01   quit-flag                     PIC X(1)  VALUE "N".
31           88   quit                                VALUE "Y".
32
33
34      PROCEDURE DIVISION.
35
36
37           PERFORM UNTIL QUIT
38
39
40               DISPLAY "   1. Add a New Customer"
41               DISPLAY "   2. Display Customer Information"
42               DISPLAY "   3. Change Customer Name"
43               DISPLAY "   4. Remove a Customer"
44               DISPLAY "   9. Exit"
45               DISPLAY "Enter option: " WITH NO ADVANCING
```

```
46                       ACCEPT option
47                       EVALUATE option
48                           WHEN 1
49                               PERFORM ADD-A-CUSTOMER
50                           WHEN 2
51                               PERFORM DISPLAY-CUSTOMER-INFO
52                           WHEN 3
53                               PERFORM CHANGE-CUSTOMER-NAME
54                           WHEN 4
55                               PERFORM REMOVE-A-CUSTOMER
56                           WHEN 9
57                               SET QUIT TO TRUE
58                       END-EVALUATE
59                   END-PERFORM
60                   STOP RUN.
61
62
63           ADD-A-CUSTOMER.
64               display "enter Customer SS number:" with no advancing
65               accept customer-ss-no-ws
66               DISPLAY "enter the customer name"
67                   WITH NO ADVANCING
68               ACCEPT customer-name-ws
69               INVOKE Customer "CreateNewCustomer"
70                   USING       customer-ss-no-ws
71                               customer-name-ws
72                   RETURNING return-data-ws
73               END-INVOKE
74               IF duplicate-number
75                   PERFORM DISPLAY-DUP-NUMBER-MESSAGE
76               ELSE
77                   IF other-problem
78                       PERFORM DISPLAY-OTHER-PROBLEM-MESSAGE
79               END-IF.
80
81
82           DISPLAY-CUSTOMER-INFO.
83               display "enter customer ss number:" with no advancing
84               accept customer-ss-no-ws
85               INVOKE Customer "RetrieveCustomer"
86                   USING       customer-ss-no-ws
87                   RETURNING   return-data-ws
88               END-INVOKE
89               set aCustomer to aCustomer-ws
90               IF customer-found
91                   INVOKE aCustomer "TellCustomerSSNo"
92                       RETURNING customer-ss-no-ws
93                   END-INVOKE
94                   DISPLAY "The Customer SS no is: ", customer-ss-no-ws
95                   INVOKE aCustomer "TellCustomerName"
96                       RETURNING customer-name-ws
97                   END-INVOKE
98                   DISPLAY "The Customer Name is: ", customer-name-ws
99               else
100                  IF no-record-found
```

```
101                    PERFORM DISPLAY-NO-ACCT-FOUND-MESSAGE
102                ELSE
103                    PERFORM DISPLAY-OTHER-PROBLEM-MESSAGE
104                END-IF
105            END-IF.
106
107
108
109        CHANGE-CUSTOMER-NAME.
110            display "enter customer ss number:" with no advancing
111            accept customer-ss-no-ws
112            INVOKE Customer "RetrieveCustomer"
113                USING        customer-ss-no-ws
114                RETURNING    return-data-ws
115            END-INVOKE
116
117
118            IF customer-found
119                display "enter name:" with no advancing
120                accept customer-name-ws
121                set aCustomer to aCustomer-ws
122                INVOKE aCustomer "ChangeCustomerName"
123                    USING        customer-name-ws
124                                 aCustomer
125                    RETURNING    return-data-ws
126                END-INVOKE
127                INVOKE aCustomer "TellCustomerName"
128                      RETURNING customer-name-ws
129                END-INVOKE
130                DISPLAY "The Revised Name is: ", customer-name-ws
131            ELSE
132                IF  no-record-found
133                    PERFORM DISPLAY-NO-ACCT-FOUND-MESSAGE
134                ELSE
135                    PERFORM DISPLAY-OTHER-PROBLEM-MESSAGE
136                END-IF
137            END-IF.
138
139
140        REMOVE-A-CUSTOMER.
141            display "enter SS number:" with no advancing
142            accept customer-ss-no-ws
143            INVOKE Customer "RetrieveCustomer"
144                USING        customer-ss-no-ws
145                RETURNING    return-data-ws
146            END-INVOKE
147            IF customer-found
148                SET aCustomer to aCustomer-ws
149                INVOKE aCustomer "RemoveCustomer"
150                    USING    aCustomer
151                RETURNING    return-data-ws
152                END-INVOKE
153            ELSE
154                IF  no-record-found
155                    PERFORM DISPLAY-NO-ACCT-FOUND-MESSAGE
```

```
156               ELSE
157                   PERFORM DISPLAY-OTHER-PROBLEM-MESSAGE
158               END-IF
159           END-IF.
160
161
162      DISPLAY-DUP-NUMBER-MESSAGE.
163          DISPLAY "A customer with this  SS number already exists"
164          Display "Press Any Key to Continue..."
165          Accept anything.
166
167
168      DISPLAY-NO-ACCT-FOUND-MESSAGE.
169          DISPLAY "This customer cannot be found"
170          Display "Press Any Key to Continue..."
171          Accept anything.
172
173
174      DISPLAY-OTHER-PROBLEM-MESSAGE.
175          DISPLAY "Unknown Problem with ISAM file.."
176          Display "Press Any Key to Continue..."
177          Accept anything.
```

CHAPTER 8:

User Interface

Thus far, you have learned how to write class programs with attributes and methods, create instances, invoke methods, and in the previous chapter, how to store and retrieve instances in a file. Although we included a simple user interface with the credit union system, it was developed with little regard to how it looked or where it was implemented. In fact, we put the user interface in the driver program. We simply wanted some way to input and output the data without distracting from the main purpose of the chapters which was to develop problem domain and data management classes.

In this chapter, our focus shifts to the all-important user interface classes. We will intentionally take a very pragmatic, simple approach to the interface—not focusing on the interface itself, but the process necessary to add an interface to our existing system. Once again, refer to the Class Layer Diagram in Figure 8.1 to help you visualize the purpose of this chapter.

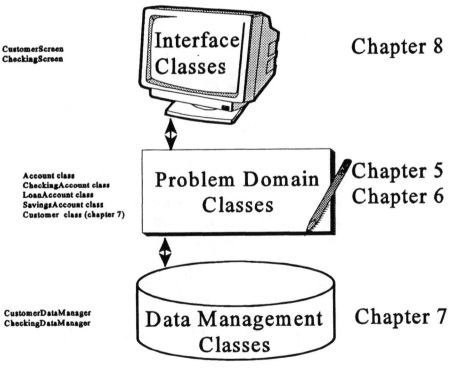

Figure 8.1 Class Layer Diagram

There are numerous interface possibilities. The user interface can utilize a variety of input and output devices such as screens, keyboards, printers, touch screens, and scanners. In this chapter, we will concentrate on the typical user interface using only a screen and keyboard. However, as you proceed through the chapter, keep in mind how the code may differ should we use a different interface such as a touch screen.

At the end of this chapter, you should have a good understanding of the process necessary to add a user interface to a system using Object COBOL and object-programming techniques. You will find that the actual code introduced in this chapter is not new—only the process used to develop the code is different. Therefore, we can focus on the process rather than the code itself. By studying this chapter, you should realize the ease with which a different physical interface could be implemented without disturbing the existing problem domain and data management classes.

DESIGNING THE USER INTERFACE

Interface design is an important component of the development process. Why? Because the user sees and interacts with the interface; it is the user's view of the system. Users could care less about what goes on "behind the screens," as long as everything is correct and fast! In this chapter, we will be concerned more with how screens can be implemented using Object COBOL rather than the actual designs themselves (although the screen designs are useful and functional). Using Object COBOL, we can implement screens in several different ways.

1. Using simple ACCEPT and DISPLAY statements to have a line driven screen.
2. Using the SCREEN SECTION to create screens and then call them when needed.
3. Using a visual programming environment, such as Visual Object COBOL or Visual BASIC, as the interface calling Object COBOL programs.

For simplicity, we are going to use the first two options: using simple ACCEPT and DISPLAY statements and a SCREEN SECTION. There are two main reasons for using these options to build the interface. First, you are probably already familiar with these statements, and you don't have to learn new COBOL code. Second, we can focus on the process of building a user interface with Object COBOL rather than concentrating on the actual procedural code.

Similar to the previous chapter, we will work with the CheckingAccount and Customer classes. (Implementation of user interfaces for the remaining classes is left as an exercise for the reader.) The main menu and a sample customer screen are provided in Figures 8.2 and 8.3, respectively. These two screens provide a good indication of the types of screens you will be developing in this chapter.

```
            1         2         3         4         5         6         7
   1234567890123456789012345678901234567890123456789012345678901234567890123456789012
 2      *******************************************************
 3                      Employees' Credit Union
 4
 5      *******************************************************
 6
 7                            Main Menu
 8
 9      *******************************************************
 0
 1                    1. Enter a New Customer
 2                    2. Display Customer Information
 3                    3. Change a Customer Name
 4                    4. Remove a Customer
 5                    5. Open a New Checking Account
 6                    6. Display Checking Account
 7                    7. Record a Check
 8                    8. Compute Service Charge
 9                    9. Close a Checking Account
 0                    0. Stop
 1
 2      *********************************************************
 3      messages go here xxxxxxxxxxxxxxxxxxxxxxxxxxxxxxxxxxxxxxxx
 4
```

Figure 8.2   Screen Layout for Main Menu

```
            1         2         3         4         5         6         7
   1234567890123456789012345678901234567890123456789012345678901234567890123456789012
 2      *******************************************************
 3                      Employees' Credit Union
 4
 5      *******************************************************
 6
 7                    Enter New Customer Screen
 8
 9      *******************************************************
 0
 1
 2          Social Security Number:  _____
 3
 4
 5          Customer Name: xxxxxxxxxxxxxxxxxxxx
 6
 7
 8      *******************************************************
 9      messages go here xxxxxxxxxxxxxxxxxxxxxxxxxxxxxxxxxxxxxxxx
 1                    Enter Y to Continue, N to Stop: _
```

Figure 8.3   Screen Layout for New Customer Entry

PROGRAM DESIGN FOR THE USER INTERFACE

Now that the screen design has been determined, we need to consider the manner in which these screens will be implemented (i.e., how we will create the code for these screens). There are several alternatives we can choose for implementing the screen design presented in the previous section. We will investigate four such options, noting the significant features of each.

OPTION 1

One option is to create a traditional procedural COBOL program responsible for displaying the menu and screens, then invoking the necessary methods in the problem domain classes. In our system, this would be a driver program, similar to what we did in earlier chapters. This option is illustrated in Figure 8.4.

However, this form constrains flexibility, should individual screens or menus need to be used by other programs. In essence, other programs would have to re-create the code needed to show the menus and screens, thus increasing duplication and associated problems of redundant code. For example, assume a new branch of the credit union only needed access to the checking account screens. A new procedural interface would have to be written to allow access to the <u>CheckingAccount</u> class (as shown in Figure 8.5). The new procedural code for the checking account screens would be a duplicate of the existing code for the menu/screens. If a change to the checking account interface were required, it would now need to be made in two places. As you can see, the duplication of code necessary with this option quickly becomes a major problem.

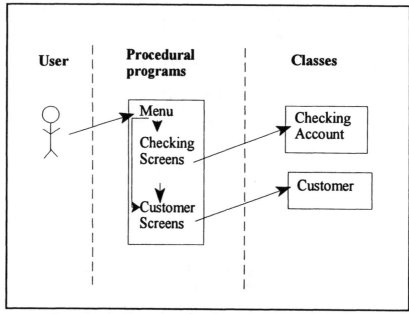

Figure 8.4   Interface Implementation—Option 1

OPTION 2

A second option is to use a procedural program for the menu and individual procedural programs for each of the screens (see Figure 8.6). This is a feasible solution that eliminates some of the problems identified in the first option. The user could now have access to the checking account through the menu or through the program written specifically for the checking account screens, resulting in more flexibility. However, specific functions of the checking account, such as opening a new account, are contained within a screen program and cannot be accessed by itself without writing additional code. Therefore, this option is more flexible than the previous option but still lacks flexibility for individual functions.

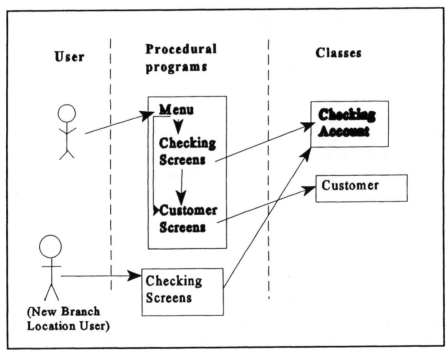

Figure 8.5   Interface Implementation—Option 1 (An Example)

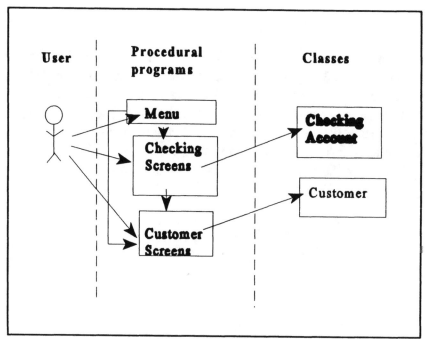

Figure 8.6   Interface Implementation—Option 2

OPTION 3

The third option is to use a procedural program for the menu and make the screens part of the Account, SavingsAccount, LoanAccount, CheckingAccount, and Customer classes, as shown in Figure 8.7. The menu would act as a driver that invokes the various methods based on specific menu choices. By doing it this way, a user uses the menu to invoke actions. Or whenever someone wants to open a checking account, for example, a message to the class is all that is needed to invoke the screen and the procedures necessary to create an account. Thus, this option provides the flexibility lacking in the previous two options.

Unfortunately, the classes are now tied to this particular user interface. In other words, we can no longer use these class programs without invoking the user interface. We have not separated the problem domain classes from the user interface classes. For example, assume a client method needs to know the balance of an account. To find the balance, it will be forced to use the user interface written for that method. Although this may not always be bad, it is a nuisance. With this option, the classes are only useful for this particular credit union application and this particular credit union. In other words, the problem domain class programs are not sufficiently generic for reuse.

OPTION 4

The fourth option calls for the creation of menu and screen classes. Each problem domain class will have an associated screen class (see Figure 8.8), similar to the approach taken with the data management classes in the previous chapter. For example, the CheckingAccount class will have an associated CheckingScreen class whose responsibility is to create the user interface for CheckingAccount. Similarly, Customer has its screen class program named CustomerScreen.

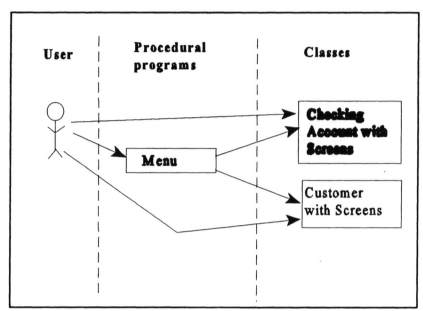

Figure 8.7   Interface Implementation—Option 3

The menu becomes a class, MenuScreen, and can easily be invoked by any client program. The menu, in turn, invokes corresponding methods in the appropriate screen classes. For example, to use the system, a driver program is written which invokes the menu. The user then chooses items from the menu to perform specific actions.

The screen methods can also be invoked without going through the menu. For example, a client program can invoke **OpenNewAccount** without using the menu. Finally, the problem domain classes, such as CheckingAccount, remain intact and unmodified, thus preserving their generic status and usefulness to other applications or other credit unions.

Overall, this solution provides the flexibility and generality not found in the other options. In addition, the use of procedural programs is eliminated, resulting in only class programs. Lastly, the problem domain classes, data management classes, and user interface classes remain separated as prescribed by the layered design technique. The system remains generic, adaptable, and maintainable. The fourth option will be used to demonstrate the user interface concepts in this chapter. Again, only the CheckingAccount and Customer classes will be implemented. The implementation of the remaining classes is straightforward.

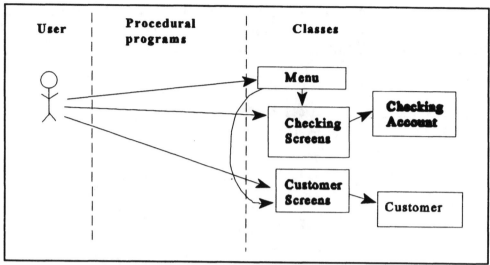

Figure 8.8   Interface Implementation—Option 4

BUILDING THE USER INTERFACE

Existing classes require no modification to implement the user interface. Both the problem domain and data management classes from the previous chapter are used here without any modification. This illustrates the independence of the user interface from the problem domain and data management classes and a significant advantage of object programming! Because the user interface is separate from the other classes, changes to the user interface will not in any way affect the other classes. We could make either a minor change, such as the wording on a screen, or more significantly, change the screen format from text-based to a graphical user interface; neither change would affect the other classes. It is not necessary here to discuss the existing problem domain and data management class programs. Each will continue to serve the same purpose as discussed in prior chapters.

THE MENUSCREEN CLASS

The MenuScreen class can be referred to as an *active object*. According to Booch's definition, an active object is "an object that can operate upon other objects, but is never operated upon by other objects" (p. 99). In this case, MenuScreen is used to invoke methods in other classes, but it takes no action of its own other than displaying the menu and passing along the user requests to the proper methods in the user interface classes. The complete MenuScreen class program is listed at the end of the chapter.

The SCREEN SECTION, shown in Figure 8.9, is used to specify the location of the menu on the screen. (The actual screen was shown earlier in Figure 8.2.) Later, we simply have to use the COBOL statement, DISPLAY, to display the menu in the format and location specified in the SCREEN SECTION.

```
                    DISPLAY MENU-SCREEN
```

```
        SCREEN SECTION.
        01  menu-screen.
            05   LINE 1  COL 12 VALUE
                 '**********************************************'.
            05   LINE 3  COL 27 VALUE 'Employees'' Credit Union'.
            05   LINE 5  COL 12 VALUE
                 '**********************************************'.
            05   LINE 7  COL 27 VALUE '        MAIN MENU'.
            05   LINE 9  COL 12 VALUE
                 '**********************************************'.


            05   LINE 10 COL 27 VALUE '1. Enter a New Customer'.
            05   LINE 11 COL 27 VALUE '2. Display Customer Information'.
            05   LINE 12 COL 27 VALUE '3. Change a Customer Name'.
            05   LINE 13 COL 27 VALUE '4. Remove a Customer'.
            05   LINE 14 COL 27 VALUE '5. Open a New Checking Account'.
            05   LINE 15 COL 27 VALUE '6. Display Checking Account'.
            05   LINE 16 COL 27 VALUE '7. Record a Check'.
            05   LINE 17 COL 27 VALUE '8. Compute Service Charge'.
            05   LINE 18 COL 27 VALUE '9. Close a Checking Account '.
            05   LINE 19 COL 27 VALUE '0. Stop'.
            05   LINE 21 COL 20 VALUE 'Selection: _'.
            05   LINE 22 COL 12 VALUE
                 '**********************************************'.
            05   LINE 23 COL 12 VALUE
                 'Message: Please Enter Your Selection 1 - 9'.
            05   LINE 24 COL 12 VALUE
                 '**********************************************'.
```

Figure 8.9 The Screen Section of MenuScreen

The only method contained in MenuScreen is **DisplayMenu**. Since this is an active object whose job is to pass along the commands to the proper class, one method is sufficient. The code for the PROCEDURE DIVISION of the **DisplayMenu** method is shown in Figure 8.10.

As shown, **DisplayMenu** accepts the users' input (after displaying the Menu-Screen), and then invokes the proper method in either CustomerScreen or CheckingScreen. Options for invoking methods in the other classes such as LoanAccount and SavingsAccount could easily be added.

```
        PROCEDURE DIVISION.
            PERFORM UNTIL QUIT
                MOVE SPACES TO option
                DISPLAY " " LINE 1 COL 1 ERASE EOS
                DISPLAY MENU-SCREEN
                ACCEPT option AT LINE 21 COL 31
                EVALUATE option
                    WHEN 1
                        INVOKE CustomerScreen "EnterNewCustomer"
                    WHEN 2
                        INVOKE CustomerScreen "DisplayCustomer"
                    WHEN 3
                        INVOKE CustomerScreen "ChangeCustomerName"
                    WHEN 4
                        INVOKE CustomerScreen "RemoveCustomer"
                    WHEN 5
                        INVOKE CheckingScreen "OpenCheckingAccount"
                    WHEN 6
                        INVOKE CheckingScreen "DisplayCheckingAccount"
                    WHEN 7
                        INVOKE CheckingScreen "RecordCheck"
                    WHEN 8
                        INVOKE CheckingScreen "ComputeServiceCharge"
                    WHEN 9
                        INVOKE CheckingScreen "CloseCheckingAccount"
                    WHEN 0
                        SET QUIT TO TRUE
                END-EVALUATE
            END-PERFORM
```

Figure 8.10 Procedure Division of DisplayMenu Method

THE CHECKINGSCREEN CLASS

The MenuScreen provides an overall user interface to the entire system. However, to access specific methods, we must use the user interface specifically established for each class. As previously mentioned, each problem domain class has an associated screen class whose responsibility is to provide a client an interface to problem domain class methods. In this section, we will look at one of the new classes necessary to implement a user interface: the CheckingScreen.

This class provides a user interface to the methods in the CheckingAccount class. First, we will look at the code for the class itself; then, we'll see how it functions as a user interface. The complete CheckingScreen class program (CH8CKSCR) is listed at the end of the chapter.

Incidentally, all of the methods in CheckingScreen are factory methods. CheckingScreen has several private methods, including **DisplayCheckingScreen**, **DisplayShallWeQuit**, **InputAccount Number**, and **InputCustomerSSNo**. It also contains several public methods:

CloseCheckingAccount,   ComputeServiceCharge,   DisplayCheckingAccount, OpenCheckingAccount, and **RecordCheck.**

Let's start by looking at the private methods. For discussion purposes, we will choose **DisplayCheckingAccount** as a representative of the private methods. The OID for displaying a checking account is shown in Figure 8.11; the code for the **DisplayCheckingAccount** is listed in Figure 8.12.

As shown in the OID, the driver program invokes **DisplayMenu** in the <u>MenuScreen</u> class (step 1) to display the menu screen. When the user chooses option 6 from the menu, the method **DisplayCheckingAccount** in <u>CheckingScreen</u> is then invoked (step 2). The next two steps needed to display the checking account information are all handled internally by the private methods **DisplayCheckingScreen** and **InputAccountNumber**. (Remember, we design the private methods to be accessible from within the owning class.)

The checking screen is then displayed (step 3), and the user enters the account number (step 4). Next, **RetrieveCheckingAccount** is invoked (step 5). If we were to trace the **RetrieveChecking Account** method inside <u>CheckingAccount</u>, we would see that it, in turn, invokes methods in <u>CheckingDataManager</u> to retrieve the checking information from the ISAM file, exactly the way we described in the previous chapter. All of this, of course, is hidden from the <u>CheckingScreen</u> class and from the end user. The checking screen is shown in Figure 8.13.

Most of the code for displaying the checking screen is straightforward and offers nothing new. By now, you should be comfortable with using the INVOKE statement. (See the **DisplayCheckingAccount** code segment or the complete <u>CheckingScreen</u> program listing at the end of the chapter.)

Note the use of the *SET* statement near the end of the PROCESS-INPUT paragraph in Figure 8.12. In this context, SET is used to assign the value of one instance pointer to another. When the customer information was retrieved, an instance pointer was returned with the *return-data-ws* data into the *anInstance-ws* area. This was pointing to the customer instance containing the data for the customer being processed. The SET is then used to properly store the pointer value in <u>aCustomer</u> so that subsequent communication with <u>aCustomer</u> will be correct. The *anInstance-ws* pointer is used as a temporary holding area for instance pointers for both customers and checking accounts. The SET statement is used to assign, in this case, the temporary pointer value to a more appropriately named data item, either <u>aCustomer</u> or <u>aCheckingAccount</u>.

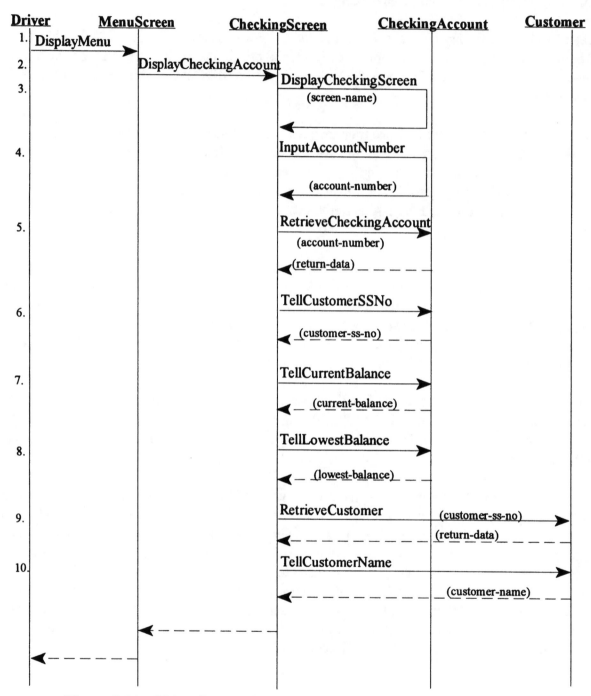

Figure 8.11   Object Interaction Diagram—DisplayCheckingAccount

```
METHOD-ID. "DisplayCheckingAccount".

WORKING-STORAGE SECTION.
01  screen-name        PIC X(30) VALUE ' DISPLAY CHECKING ACCOUNT'.

PROCEDURE DIVISION.
    MOVE SPACES TO shall-we-quit-sw
    PERFORM PROCESS-INPUT
        UNTIL quit-indicated.
    EXIT METHOD.

PROCESS-INPUT.
    INVOKE Self "DisplayCheckingScreen"
        USING screen-name
    END-INVOKE
    MOVE SPACES TO switches
    PERFORM INPUT-ACCOUNT-NUMBER
        UNTIL quit-indicated OR valid-input
    IF NOT quit-indicated
        INVOKE anAccount "TellCustomerSSNo"
            RETURNING customer-ss-no-ws
        INVOKE anAccount "TellCurrentBalance"
            RETURNING current-balance-ws
        INVOKE anAccount "TellLowestBalance"
            RETURNING lowest-balance-ws
        MOVE current-balance-ws TO edited-current-balance-ws
        MOVE lowest-balance-ws  TO edited-lowest-balance-ws
        DISPLAY customer-ss-no-ws
            AT LINE 13 COL 42 ERASE EOL
        DISPLAY edited-current-balance-ws
            AT LINE 17 COL 35 ERASE EOL
        DISPLAY edited-lowest-balance-ws
            AT LINE 19 COL 35 ERASE EOL
        INVOKE Customer "RetrieveCustomer"
            USING       customer-ss-no-ws
            RETURNING   return-data-ws
        END-INVOKE
        IF record-found
            SET aCustomer TO anInstance-ws
            INVOKE aCustomer "TellCustomerName"
                RETURNING customer-name-ws
            END-INVOKE
            DISPLAY customer-name-ws AT LINE 15 COL 33 ERASE EOL
        END-IF
        INVOKE "DisplayShallWeQuit"
    END-IF.

INPUT-ACCOUNT-NUMBER.
    INVOKE Self "InputAccountNumber" RETURNING account-number-ws
    IF NOT quit-indicated
        INVOKE CheckingAccount "RetrieveCheckingAccount"
            USING       account-number-ws
            RETURNING   return-data-ws
        END-INVOKE
        IF record-found
            MOVE 'YES' TO valid-input-switch
        ELSE
            MOVE 'NO' TO valid-input-switch
            DISPLAY
            'This Account Number found, please re-enter'
                AT LINE 23 COL 12 ERASE EOS
            END-DISPLAY
            INVOKE Self "DisplayShallWeQuit"
        END-IF
    END-IF.


END METHOD "DisplayCheckingAccount".
```

Figure 8.12   DisplayCheckingAccount Method

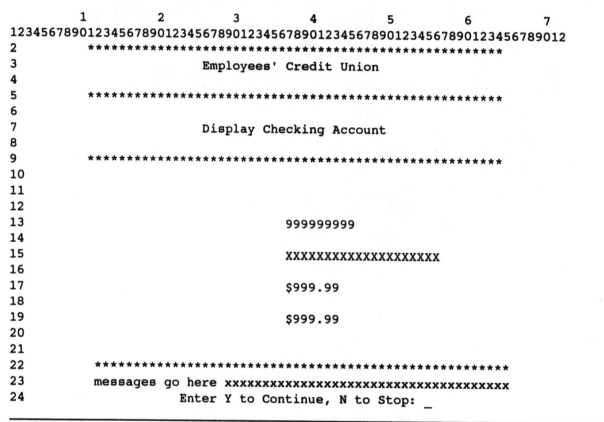

Figure 8.13   Display Checking Account Screen

Another of the public methods available in <u>CheckingScreen</u> is **ComputeServiceCharge**. This method provides the user interface needed to compute the service charge for a checking account. The OID for this method is shown in Figure 8.14, and the source code is shown in Figure 8.15.

At this point, you should have noticed something familiar about this method. That's right—we already have a method called **ComputeServiceCharge** in the <u>CheckingAccount</u> class. Have we made a mistake? No. It is possible to have the same method name in two or more different classes. In many cases, this is preferred. In this case, we are using the **ComputeServiceCharge** differently in the two classes: in the <u>CheckingScreen</u> class, the method is used to provide the user interface; in the <u>CheckingAccount</u> class, the method is used to calculate the service charge. This use of the same name makes it easier for us to remember which method to invoke to compute the service charge. In other words, regardless of whether we are using the user interface or going directly to the class, the method name is **ComputeServiceCharge**. We only have to remember the target class and the parameters to supply. This, of course, is yet another example of polymorphic methods.

The OID in Figure 8.14 maps the actions caused by invoking **ComputeServiceCharge.** The <u>CheckingScreen</u> displays the checking screen (private method), accepts the account number

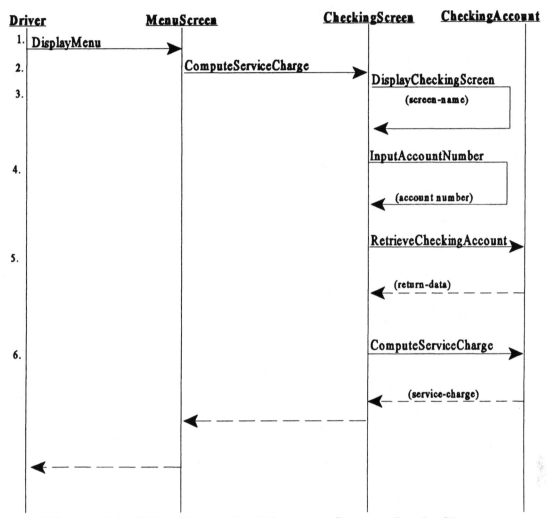

Figure 8.14   Object Interaction Diagram—ComputeServiceCharge

```
METHOD-ID. "ComputeServiceCharge".
WORKING-STORAGE SECTION.
01  screen-name      PIC X(30) VALUE '  COMPUTE SERVICE CHARGE'.

PROCEDURE DIVISION.
    MOVE SPACES TO shall-we-quit-sw
    PERFORM PROCESS-INPUT
        UNTIL quit-indicated.
    EXIT METHOD.          .

PROCESS-INPUT.
    INVOKE Self "DisplayCheckingScreen"
        USING screen-name
    END-INVOKE
    MOVE SPACES TO switches
    PERFORM INPUT-ACCOUNT-NUMBER
        UNTIL quit-indicated OR valid-input
    IF NOT quit-indicated
        INVOKE anAccount "ComputeServiceCharge"
            RETURNING service-charge-ws
        MOVE service-charge-ws TO edited-service-charge-ws
        DISPLAY SPACE AT LINE 13 ERASE EOS
        DISPLAY "Amount of Service Charge" AT LINE 21 COL 18
        DISPLAY edited-service-charge-ws
            AT LINE 21 COL 44
        INVOKE "DisplayShallWeQuit"
    END-IF.

INPUT-ACCOUNT-NUMBER.
    INVOKE Self "InputAccountNumber" RETURNING account-number-ws
    IF NOT quit-indicated
        INVOKE CheckingAccount "RetrieveCheckingAccount"
            USING        account-number-ws
            RETURNING    return-data-ws
        END-INVOKE
        IF record-found
            MOVE 'YES' TO valid-input-switch
        ELSE
            MOVE 'NO' TO valid-input-switch
            DISPLAY
            'This Account Number found, please re-enter'
                AT LINE 23 COL 12 ERASE EOS
            END-DISPLAY
            INVOKE Self "DisplayShallWeQuit"
        END-IF
    END-IF.

END METHOD "ComputeServiceCharge".
```

Figure 8.15 ComputeServiceCharge Method

from the user (private method), and then retrieves the checking account information from CheckingAccount. Finally, **ComputeServiceCharge** is invoked in CheckingAccount (step 6). Thus, the **ComputeServiceCharge** message sent from the MenuScreen causes the user interface to be invoked, whereas the **ComputeServiceCharge** message sent from the CheckingScreen to CheckingAccount causes the service charge to be calculated and returned. As seen here, polymorphism, when used properly, can be a very useful technique for developing class programs. Incidentally, we have two additional polymorphic methods in CheckingScreen: **CloseCheckingAccount** and **OpenCheckingAccount**.

THE CUSTOMERSCREEN CLASS

The CustomerScreen class is built very much like CheckingScreen. Polymorphic methods, such as **ChangeCustomerName** and **RemoveCustomer**, provide a consistent interface with the Customer class. Private methods, such as **DisplayCustomerScreen** and **InputCustomerName**, are used internally by the CustomerScreen class to provide a user interface. The complete source code for the CustomerScreen class program is provided at the end of the chapter.

OBJECT PROGRAMMING AT ITS FINEST—EASY MAINTENANCE

In this chapter, we have demonstrated the construction of user interface classes. In this case, we built text-based screens using the traditional COBOL statements ACCEPT and DISPLAY. However, let's assume that we want to change to a GUI. To the rest of the system, the change would be hidden. We only need to change the user interface classes—MenuScreen, CheckingScreen, and CustomerScreen. The original problem domain and data management classes are unaffected. The method interfaces stay the same, and so the client program never knows that the user interface class has been significantly changed (from a programming perspective). A change to a GUI interface is localized to only a few objects, thus protecting existing (and perhaps widely used) classes from exposure to problems involved with changing source code. This is object programming at its finest—changes are localized and hidden.

SUMMARY

The classes and their respective method interfaces developed in this chapter are summarized at the end of the chapter. Since existing problem domain and data management classes were not changed, we have not reintroduced them here. At this point, we have a complete working credit union system consisting of user interface, problem domain, and data management classes.

This chapter has focused on the development of the user interface classes. Although no new coding statements were necessary in this chapter, the process in which the user interface is developed is important. The separation of the user interface layer from the problem domain and data management layer allows the system to be both flexible and maintainable. We have seen how a few simple classes can add the user interface necessary for both the CheckingAccount and Customer classes.

In this chapter, we developed a simple text-based interface consisting of a few screens. Typical ACCEPT and DISPLAY statements were used to implement the interface. However, a GUI could also have been used using the same process as presented in this chapter. In many cases, the COBOL compiler is supplied with a class library containing various screen classes, including GUI classes. The reuse of these class programs can dramatically reduce the effort to develop elaborate user interfaces.

KEY TERMS

Active object
SET

REVIEW QUESTIONS

1. Why is it important to separate the problem domain classes from the user interface classes? What problems can result from not separating them?

2. Why was the menu presented as a separate class (MenuScreen)? What are some other options for implementing a menu (without creating a new class)?

3. What Object COBOL verb is used to assign the value of one instance pointer to another? Why would it be necessary to set two pointers to the same instance?

4. Is it possible for two different classes to have methods by the same name? Can a class have two methods with the same name?

EXERCISES

1. Develop the classes necessary to produce a user interface for the LoanAccount class.

2. Create GUI screens for the Customer class.

BIBLIOGRAPHY

Booch, G. <u>Object-Oriented Analysis and Design with Applications</u>. Benjamin-Cummings, 1994.

Brown, D. <u>An Introduction to Object-Oriented Analysis</u>. John Wiley & Sons, 1997.

Coad, P., and Yourdon, E. <u>Object-Oriented Analysis</u>. Yourdon Press, Prentice-Hall, 1991.

Jacobson, I., et al. <u>Object-Oriented Software Engineering: A Use Case Driven Approach</u>. Addison-Wesley, 1992.

Taylor, D. A. <u>Object-Oriented Systems: Planning and Implementation</u>. John Wiley & Sons, 1992.

CLASS DESCRIPTIONS

1. **CH8-MENU** is a class program for <u>MenuScreen.</u>
   Attributes: none
   Factory Method:
   ```
   DisplayMenu.
   ```
   Instance Methods: none

2. **CH8CKSCR** is a class program for CheckingScreen.
   Attributes: none
   Factory Methods:
   ```
   CloseCheckingAccount
   ComputeServiceCharge
   DisplayCheckingAccount
   <private> DisplayCheckingScreen   USING screen-name
   <private> DisplayShallWeQuit
   <private> InputAccountNumber       RETURNING account-number
   <private> InputCustomerSSNo        RETURNING customer-ss-no
   OpenCheckingAccount
   RecordCheck
   ```
   Instance Methods: none

3. **CH8CUSCR** is a class program for CustomerScreen.
   Attributes: none
   Factory Methods:
   ```
   ChangeCustomerName
   EnterNewCustomer
   DisplayCustomer
   <private> DisplayCustomerScreen   USING screen-name
   <private> DisplayShallWeQuit
   <private> InputCustomerName        RETURNING customer-name
   <private> InputCustomerSSNo        RETURNING customer-ss-no
   RemoveCustomer
   ```
   Instance Methods: none

PROGRAM LISTINGS

Driver Program

```
*   CH8-PRG1 is a procedural program designed to
*     INVOKE DisplayMenu method in MenuScreen class
*-----------------------------------------------------------
```

```
1      PROGRAM-ID. CH8-PRG1.
2
3      CLASS-CONTROL.
4          MenuScreen   is class "CH8-MENU".
5
6      PROCEDURE DIVISION.
7          INVOKE MenuScreen "DisplayMenu"
8          STOP RUN.
```

MenuScreen Program

```
*   CH8-MENU is the class program for MenuScreen class
*    This class displays the main menu and accepts selections
*-------------------------------------------------------------
```

```
1        CLASS-ID. CH8-MENU.
2
3        CLASS-CONTROL.
4            Menu                is class "CH8-MENU"
5            CustomerScreen      is class "CH8CUSCR"
6            CheckingScreen      is class "CH8CKSCR".
7
8        CLASS-OBJECT.
9
10       *-------------------------------------------------------------
11       * DisplayMenu displays the system menu & accepts the selection
12       *-------------------------------------------------------------
13
14       METHOD-ID. "DisplayMenu".
15
16       WORKING-STORAGE SECTION.
17
18       01   option                   PIC X(1).
19       01   quit-flag                PIC X(1)  VALUE "N".
20            88   quit                           VALUE "Y".
21
22       SCREEN SECTION.
23       01   menu-screen.
24            05   LINE 1  COL 12 VALUE
25            '*********************************************************'.
26            05   LINE 3  COL 27 VALUE 'Employees'' Credit Union'.
27            05   LINE 5  COL 12 VALUE
28            '*********************************************************'.
29            05   LINE 7  COL 27 VALUE '        MAIN MENU'.
30            05   LINE 9  COL 12 VALUE
31            '*********************************************************'.
32
33            05   LINE 10 COL 27 VALUE '1. Enter a New Customer'.
34            05   LINE 11 COL 27 VALUE '2. Display Customer Information'.
35            05   LINE 12 COL 27 VALUE '3. Change a Customer Name'.
36            05   LINE 13 COL 27 VALUE '4. Remove a Customer'.
37            05   LINE 14 COL 27 VALUE '5. Open a New Checking Account'.
38            05   LINE 15 COL 27 VALUE '6. Display Checking Account'.
39            05   LINE 16 COL 27 VALUE '7. Record a Check'.
40            05   LINE 17 COL 27 VALUE '8. Compute Service Charge'.
41            05   LINE 18 COL 27 VALUE '9. Close a Checking Account '.
42            05   LINE 19 COL 27 VALUE '0. Stop'.
43            05   LINE 21 COL 20 VALUE 'Selection: _'.
44            05   LINE 22 COL 12 VALUE
45            '*********************************************************'.
46            05   LINE 23 COL 12 VALUE
47            'Message: Please Enter Your Selection 1 - 9'.
48            05   LINE 24 COL 12 VALUE
```

```
49                  '****************************************************'.
50
51
52          PROCEDURE DIVISION.
53              PERFORM UNTIL QUIT
54                  MOVE SPACES TO option
55                  DISPLAY " " LINE 1 COL 1 ERASE EOS
56                  DISPLAY MENU-SCREEN
57                  ACCEPT option AT LINE 21 COL 31
58                  EVALUATE option
59                      WHEN 1
60                          INVOKE CustomerScreen "EnterNewCustomer"
61                      WHEN 2
62                          INVOKE CustomerScreen "DisplayCustomer"
63                      WHEN 3
64                          INVOKE CustomerScreen "ChangeCustomerName"
65                      WHEN 4
66                          INVOKE CustomerScreen "RemoveCustomer"
67                      WHEN 5
68                          INVOKE CheckingScreen "OpenCheckingAccount"
69                      WHEN 6
70                          INVOKE CheckingScreen "DisplayCheckingAccount"
71                      WHEN 7
72                          INVOKE CheckingScreen "RecordCheck"
73                      WHEN 8
74                          INVOKE CheckingScreen "ComputeServiceCharge"
75                      WHEN 9
76                          INVOKE CheckingScreen "CloseCheckingAccount"
77                      WHEN 0
78                          SET QUIT TO TRUE
79                  END-EVALUATE
80              END-PERFORM
81              EXIT METHOD.
82
83          END METHOD "DisplayMenu".
84          END CLASS-OBJECT.
85
86          END CLASS CH8-MENU.
```

CheckingScreen Program

```
*   CH8CKSCR is a class program for CheckingScreen which is a
*     class designed to do all screen I/O for CheckingAccount class
*     Public Factory Methods are:
*     1. ComputeServiceCharge
*     2. CloseCheckingAccount
*     3. DisplayCheckingAccount
*     4. OpenCheckingAccount
*     5. RecordCheck
*     Private Factory Methods are:
*     1. DisplayCheckingScreen
*     2. DisplayShallWeQuit
*     3. InputAccountNumber
*     4. InputCustomerSSNo
*
*-------------------------------------------------------------
```

```
 1        CLASS-ID.  CH8CKSCR.
 2
 3        CLASS-CONTROL.
 4            CheckingScreen      is class "CH8CKSCR"
 5            Customer            is class "CH7-CUST"
 6            CheckingAccount     is class "CH7-CHEK".
 7
 8        CLASS-OBJECT.
 9
10        01  switches.
11            05  valid-input-switch      PIC X(3).
12                88  valid-input         VALUE 'YES'.
13            05  shall-we-quit-sw            PIC X(1).
14                88  valid-response      VALUES 'C' 'c' 'S' 's'.
15                88  quit-indicated      VALUES 'S' 's'.
16
17        01  account-number-ws           PIC 9(5).
18        01  amount-of-check-ws          PIC 9(5)V99.
19        01  current-balance-ws          PIC S9(5)V99.
20        01  edited-current-balance-ws   PIC $zz,zz9.99-.
21        01  lowest-balance-ws           PIC S9(5)V99.
22        01  edited-lowest-balance-ws    PIC $zz,zz9.99-.
23        01  customer-ss-no-ws           PIC 9(9).
24        01  customer-name-ws            PIC X(20).
25        01  service-charge-ws           Pic 9(4)V99.
26        01  edited-service-charge-ws    PIC $z,zz9.99-.
27        01  anAccount           USAGE IS OBJECT REFERENCE.
28        01  aCustomer           USAGE IS OBJECT REFERENCE.
29
30        01  return-data-ws.
31            05  return-code-ws              PIC X(3).
32                88  no-record-found     VALUE "NRF".
33                88  duplicate-number    VALUE "DUP".
34                88  other-problem       VALUE "BAD".
35                88  record-found        VALUE "OK".
36            05  anInstance-ws       USAGE IS OBJECT REFERENCE.
37
```

```
38     *------ Public Factory Methods --------------------------------
39
40
41      METHOD-ID. "ComputeServiceCharge".
42      WORKING-STORAGE SECTION.
43      01  screen-name      PIC X(30) VALUE '  COMPUTE SERVICE CHARGE'.
44
45      PROCEDURE DIVISION.
46          MOVE SPACES TO shall-we-quit-sw
47          PERFORM PROCESS-INPUT
48              UNTIL quit-indicated.
49          EXIT METHOD.
50
51      PROCESS-INPUT.
52          INVOKE Self "DisplayCheckingScreen"
53              USING screen-name
54          END-INVOKE
55          MOVE SPACES TO switches
56          PERFORM INPUT-ACCOUNT-NUMBER
57              UNTIL quit-indicated OR valid-input
58          IF NOT quit-indicated
59              INVOKE anAccount "ComputeServiceCharge"
60                  RETURNING service-charge-ws
61              MOVE service-charge-ws TO edited-service-charge-ws
62              DISPLAY SPACE AT LINE 13 ERASE EOS
63              DISPLAY "Amount of Service Charge" AT LINE 21 COL 18
64              DISPLAY edited-service-charge-ws
65                  AT LINE 21 COL 44
66              INVOKE "DisplayShallWeQuit"
67          END-IF.
68
69      INPUT-ACCOUNT-NUMBER.
70          INVOKE Self "InputAccountNumber" RETURNING account-number-ws
71          IF NOT quit-indicated
72              INVOKE CheckingAccount "RetrieveCheckingAccount"
73                  USING       account-number-ws
74                  RETURNING   return-data-ws
75              END-INVOKE
76              IF record-found
77                  MOVE 'YES' TO valid-input-switch
78              ELSE
79                  MOVE 'NO' TO valid-input-switch
80                  DISPLAY
81                  'This Account Number found, please re-enter'
82                      AT LINE 23 COL 12 ERASE EOS
83                  END-DISPLAY
84                  INVOKE Self "DisplayShallWeQuit"
85              END-IF
86          END-IF.
87
88      END METHOD "ComputeServiceCharge".
89
90      *-----------------------------------------------------------
91
92      METHOD-ID. "CloseCheckingAccount".
93
94      WORKING-STORAGE SECTION.
```

```
95        01   screen-name PIC X(30) VALUE 'CLOSE CHECKING ACCOUNT SCREEN'.
96
97        PROCEDURE DIVISION.
98            MOVE SPACES TO switches
99            PERFORM PROCESS-INPUT
100               UNTIL quit-indicated.
101           EXIT METHOD.
102
103       PROCESS-INPUT.
104           INVOKE Self "DisplayCheckingScreen"
105               USING screen-name
106           END-INVOKE
107           MOVE SPACES TO switches
108           PERFORM INPUT-ACCOUNT-NUMBER
109               UNTIL quit-indicated OR valid-input
110           IF NOT quit-indicated
111               INVOKE anAccount "TellCustomerSSNo"
112                   RETURNING customer-ss-no-ws
113               INVOKE anAccount "TellCurrentBalance"
114                   RETURNING current-balance-ws
115               INVOKE anAccount "TellLowestBalance"
116                   RETURNING lowest-balance-ws
117               MOVE current-balance-ws TO edited-current-balance-ws
118               MOVE lowest-balance-ws  TO edited-lowest-balance-ws
119               DISPLAY customer-ss-no-ws
120                   AT LINE 13 COL 42 ERASE EOL
121               DISPLAY edited-current-balance-ws
122                   AT LINE 17 COL 35 ERASE EOL
123               DISPLAY edited-lowest-balance-ws
124                   AT LINE 19 COL 35 ERASE EOL
125               INVOKE Customer "RetrieveCustomer"
126                   USING      customer-ss-no-ws
127                   RETURNING  return-data-ws
128               END-INVOKE
129               IF record-found
130                   SET aCustomer TO anInstance-ws
131                   INVOKE aCustomer "TellCustomerName"
132                       RETURNING customer-name-ws
133                   END-INVOKE
134                   DISPLAY customer-name-ws AT LINE 15 COL 33 ERASE EOL
135               END-IF
136
137               DISPLAY 'Do You Want to Close This Account?'
138                   AT LINE 23 COL 12 ERASE EOS
139               INVOKE Self "DisplayShallWeQuit"
140               IF NOT quit-indicated
141                   INVOKE anAccount "CloseCheckingAccount"
142                       USING      anAccount
143                       RETURNING  return-data-ws
144                   DISPLAY 'This Account has been Closed'
145                       AT LINE 23 COL 12 ERASE EOS
146               ELSE
147                   DISPLAY 'This Account has NOT been Closed'
148                       AT LINE 23 COL 12 ERASE EOS
149               END-IF
150               INVOKE Self "DisplayShallWeQuit"
151           END-IF.
```

```
152    INPUT-ACCOUNT-NUMBER.
153        INVOKE Self "InputAccountNumber" RETURNING account-number-ws
154        IF NOT quit-indicated
155            INVOKE CheckingAccount "RetrieveCheckingAccount"
156                USING        account-number-ws
157                RETURNING    return-data-ws
158            END-INVOKE
159            IF record-found
160                MOVE 'YES' TO valid-input-switch
161            ELSE
162                MOVE 'NO' TO valid-input-switch
163                DISPLAY
164                'This Account Number found, please re-enter'
165                    AT LINE 23 COL 12 ERASE EOS
166                END-DISPLAY
167                INVOKE Self "DisplayShallWeQuit"
168            END-IF
169        END-IF.
170
171    END METHOD "CloseCheckingAccount".
172
173    *-------------------------------------------------------------
174
175    METHOD-ID. "DisplayCheckingAccount".
176
177    WORKING-STORAGE SECTION.
178    01   screen-name      PIC X(30) VALUE '  DISPLAY CHECKING ACCOUNT'.
179
180    PROCEDURE DIVISION.
181        MOVE SPACES TO shall-we-quit-sw
182        PERFORM PROCESS-INPUT
183            UNTIL quit-indicated.
184        EXIT METHOD.
185
186    PROCESS-INPUT.
187        INVOKE Self "DisplayCheckingScreen"
188            USING screen-name
189        END-INVOKE
190        MOVE SPACES TO switches
191        PERFORM INPUT-ACCOUNT-NUMBER
192            UNTIL quit-indicated OR valid-input
193        IF NOT quit-indicated
194            INVOKE anAccount "TellCustomerSSNo"
195                RETURNING customer-ss-no-ws
196            INVOKE anAccount "TellCurrentBalance"
197                RETURNING current-balance-ws
198            INVOKE anAccount "TellLowestBalance"
199                RETURNING lowest-balance-ws
200            MOVE current-balance-ws TO edited-current-balance-ws
201            MOVE lowest-balance-ws  TO edited-lowest-balance-ws
202            DISPLAY customer-ss-no-ws
203                AT LINE 13 COL 42 ERASE EOL
204            DISPLAY edited-current-balance-ws
205                AT LINE 17 COL 35 ERASE EOL
206            DISPLAY edited-lowest-balance-ws
207                AT LINE 19 COL 35 ERASE EOL
208            INVOKE Customer "RetrieveCustomer"
```

```
209                     USING      customer-ss-no-ws
210                     RETURNING    return-data-ws
211                 END-INVOKE
212                 IF record-found
213                     SET aCustomer TO anInstance-ws
214                     INVOKE aCustomer "TellCustomerName"
215                         RETURNING customer-name-ws
216                     END-INVOKE
217                     DISPLAY customer-name-ws AT LINE 15 COL 33 ERASE EOL
218                 END-IF
219                 INVOKE "DisplayShallWeQuit"
220             END-IF.
221
222         INPUT-ACCOUNT-NUMBER.
223             INVOKE Self "InputAccountNumber" RETURNING account-number-ws
224             IF NOT quit-indicated
225                 INVOKE CheckingAccount "RetrieveCheckingAccount"
226                     USING      account-number-ws
227                     RETURNING    return-data-ws
228                 END-INVOKE
229                 IF record-found
230                     MOVE 'YES' TO valid-input-switch
231                 ELSE
232                     MOVE 'NO' TO valid-input-switch
233                     DISPLAY
234                     'This Account Number found, please re-enter'
235                         AT LINE 23 COL 12 ERASE EOS
236                     END-DISPLAY
237                     INVOKE Self "DisplayShallWeQuit"
238                 END-IF
239             END-IF.
240
241         END METHOD "DisplayCheckingAccount".
242
243         *-------------------------------------------------------------
244
245         METHOD-ID. "OpenCheckingAccount".
246
247         WORKING-STORAGE SECTION.
248         01  screen-name PIC X(30) VALUE 'OPEN CHECKING ACCOUNT SCREEN'.
249
250         PROCEDURE DIVISION.
251             MOVE SPACES TO switches
252             PERFORM PROCESS-INPUT
253                 UNTIL quit-indicated
254             EXIT METHOD.
255
256         PROCESS-INPUT.
257             INVOKE Self "DisplayCheckingScreen"  USING screen-name
258             MOVE SPACES TO switches
259             PERFORM INPUT-ACCOUNT-NUMBER
260                 UNTIL quit-indicated OR valid-input
261             IF NOT quit-indicated
262                 INVOKE CheckingAccount "RetrieveCheckingAccount"
263                     USING      account-number-ws
264                     RETURNING    return-data-ws
265                 END-INVOKE
```

```
266            MOVE SPACES TO switches
267            PERFORM INPUT-CUSTOMER-SS-NO
268                UNTIL valid-input OR quit-indicated
269            IF NOT quit-indicated
270                SET aCustomer TO anInstance-ws
271                INVOKE aCustomer "TellCustomerName"
272                    RETURNING customer-name-ws
273                END-INVOKE
274                DISPLAY customer-name-ws AT LINE 15 COL 33
275                MOVE SPACES TO switches
276                PERFORM INPUT-CURRENT-BALANCE
277                    UNTIL valid-input OR quit-indicated
278                IF NOT quit-indicated
279                    INVOKE anAccount "OpenNewAccount"
280                        USING account-number-ws, customer-ss-no-ws
281                        RETURNING return-data-ws
282                    END-INVOKE
283                END-IF
284            END-IF
285        END-IF.
286
287    INPUT-ACCOUNT-NUMBER.
288        INVOKE Self "InputAccountNumber" RETURNING account-number-ws
289        IF NOT quit-indicated
290            INVOKE CheckingAccount "RetrieveCheckingAccount"
291                USING       account-number-ws
292                RETURNING   return-data-ws
293            END-INVOKE
294            IF no-record-found
295                MOVE 'YES' TO valid-input-switch
296            ELSE
297                MOVE 'NO' TO valid-input-switch
298                DISPLAY
299                'Duplicate Account Number found, please re-enter'
300                    AT LINE 23 COL 12 ERASE EOS
301                END-DISPLAY
302                INVOKE Self "DisplayShallWeQuit"
303            END-IF
304        END-IF.
305
306    INPUT-CURRENT-BALANCE.
307        DISPLAY 'Enter the Current Balance'
308            AT LINE 23 COL 12 ERASE EOL
309        ACCEPT current-balance-ws AT LINE 17 COL 35
310        IF current-balance-ws NUMERIC
311            MOVE 'YES' TO valid-input-switch
312        ELSE
313            DISPLAY 'Current Balance is not Numeric, Please Re-enter'
314                AT LINE 23 COL 12 ERASE EOS
315            INVOKE Self "DisplayShallWeQuit"
316        END-IF.
317
318    INPUT-CUSTOMER-SS-NO.
319        INVOKE Self "InputCustomerSSNo" RETURNING customer-ss-no-ws
320        IF NOT quit-indicated
321            INVOKE Customer "RetrieveCustomer"
322                USING       customer-ss-no-ws
```

```
323                     RETURNING   return-data-ws
324               END-INVOKE
325               IF no-record-found
326                   MOVE 'YES' TO valid-input-switch
327               ELSE
328                   MOVE 'NO' TO valid-input-switch
329                   DISPLAY
330                   'Duplicate SS Number found, please re-enter'
331                       AT LINE 23 COL 12 ERASE EOS
332                   END-DISPLAY
333                   INVOKE Self "DisplayShallWeQuit"
334               END-IF
335           END-IF.
336
337       END METHOD "OpenCheckingAccount".
338
339
340
341       *-------------------------------------------------------
342
343       METHOD-ID. "RecordCheck".
344
345       WORKING-STORAGE SECTION.
346       01   screen-name     PIC X(30) VALUE '  RECORD CHECK'.
347
348       PROCEDURE DIVISION.
349           MOVE SPACES TO shall-we-quit-sw
350           PERFORM PROCESS-INPUT
351               UNTIL quit-indicated.
352           EXIT METHOD.
353
354       PROCESS-INPUT.
355           INVOKE Self "DisplayCheckingScreen" USING screen-name
356           MOVE SPACES TO switches
357           PERFORM INPUT-ACCOUNT-NUMBER
358               UNTIL quit-indicated OR valid-input
359           IF NOT quit-indicated
360               MOVE SPACES TO switches
361               PERFORM INPUT-AMOUNT-OF-CHECK
362                   UNTIL quit-indicated OR valid-input
363               IF NOT quit-indicated
364                   INVOKE anAccount "RecordCheck" USING anAccount,
365                                                   amount-of-check-ws
366                   INVOKE anAccount "TellCurrentBalance"
367                       RETURNING current-balance-ws
368                   MOVE current-balance-ws TO edited-current-balance-ws
369                   DISPLAY edited-current-balance-ws
370                       AT LINE 17 COL 35 ERASE EOL
371               END-IF
372               INVOKE "DisplayShallWeQuit"
373           END-IF.
374
375       INPUT-ACCOUNT-NUMBER.
376           INVOKE Self "InputAccountNumber" RETURNING account-number-ws
377           IF NOT quit-indicated
378               INVOKE CheckingAccount "RetrieveCheckingAccount"
379                   USING        account-number-ws
```

```
380                           RETURNING    return-data-ws
381                     END-INVOKE
382                 IF record-found
383                     MOVE 'YES' TO valid-input-switch
384                 ELSE
385                     MOVE 'NO' TO valid-input-switch
386                     DISPLAY
387                     'This Account Number found, please re-enter'
388                         AT LINE 23 COL 12 ERASE EOS
389                     END-DISPLAY
390                     INVOKE Self "DisplayShallWeQuit"
391                 END-IF
392             END-IF.
393
394     INPUT-AMOUNT-OF-CHECK.
395         DISPLAY 'Amount of Check:' AT LINE 13 COL 18 ERASE EOS
396         DISPLAY
397             'Enter The Check Amount' AT LINE 23 COL 12 ERASE EOS
398         MOVE SPACES TO switches
399         PERFORM
400             UNTIL valid-input OR quit-indicated
401             ACCEPT amount-of-check-ws AT LINE 13 COL 35
402             IF amount-of-check-ws NUMERIC
403                 MOVE 'YES' TO valid-input-switch
404             ELSE
405                 DISPLAY
406                     'The Check Amount not numeric, please re-enter'
407                         AT LINE 23 COL 12 ERASE EOS
408                 END-DISPLAY
409                 INVOKE Self "DisplayShallWeQuit"
410             END-IF
411         END-PERFORM.
412
413     END METHOD "RecordCheck".
414
415 *------ Private Factory Methods ---------------------------
416
417     METHOD-ID. "DisplayCheckingScreen".
418
419     LINKAGE SECTION.
420     01  SCREEN-NAME      PIC X(30).
421
422     SCREEN SECTION.
423     01  checking-screen.
424         05  LINE 1  COL 12 VALUE
425             '*****************************************************'.
426         05  LINE 3  COL 27 VALUE 'Employees'' Credit Union'.
427         05  LINE 5  COL 12 VALUE
428             '*****************************************************'.
429         05  PIC X(30) FROM SCREEN-NAME LINE 7  COL 26.
430         05  LINE 9  COL 12 VALUE
431             '*****************************************************'.
432         05  LINE 11 COL 18 VALUE 'Account Number: _____'.
433         05  LINE 13 COL 18 VALUE 'Social Security Number: _____'.
434         05  LINE 15 COL 18 VALUE 'Customer Name:' .
435         05  LINE 17 COL 18 VALUE 'Current Balance: _____'.
436         05  LINE 22 COL 12 VALUE
```

```
437                 '****************************************************'.
438
439        PROCEDURE DIVISION  USING screen-name.
440
441            DISPLAY " " LINE 1 COL 1 ERASE EOS
442            DISPLAY checking-screen
443            EXIT METHOD.
444
445        END METHOD "DisplayCheckingScreen".
446
447        *-------------------------------------------------------------
448
449        METHOD-ID. "DisplayShallWeQuit".
450
451        PROCEDURE DIVISION.
452
453            MOVE SPACES TO shall-we-quit-sw
454            PERFORM UNTIL VALID-RESPONSE
455                DISPLAY "              Enter C to Continue, S to Stop: _"
456                    AT LINE 24 COL 12 ERASE EOS
457                    ACCEPT shall-we-quit-sw LINE 24 COL 55
458            END-PERFORM.
459
460
461        END METHOD "DisplayShallWeQuit".
462
463        *-------------------------------------------------------------
464
465        METHOD-ID. "InputAccountNumber".
466
467        LINKAGE SECTION.
468        01  account-number-ls              PIC 9(5).
469
470        PROCEDURE DIVISION RETURNING account-number-ls.
471            DISPLAY
472                'Message: Enter The Account Number'
473                    LINE 23 COL 12 ERASE EOS
474            END-DISPLAY
475
476            MOVE SPACES TO switches
477            PERFORM ACCEPT-ACCOUNT-NUMBER
478                UNTIL valid-input OR quit-indicated
479            EXIT METHOD.
480
481        ACCEPT-ACCOUNT-NUMBER.
482            MOVE ZEROS TO account-number-ls
483            ACCEPT account-number-ls AT LINE 11 COL 34
484            IF account-number-ls NUMERIC
485                MOVE 'YES' TO valid-input-switch
486            ELSE
487                DISPLAY
488                    'Account Number not numeric, please re-enter'
489                    AT LINE 23 COL 12 ERASE EOS
490                END-DISPLAY
491                INVOKE Self "DisplayShallWeQuit"
492            END-IF
493
```

```
494      END METHOD "InputAccountNumber".
495
496      *-----------------------------------------------------------
497
498      METHOD-ID. "InputCustomerSSNo".
499
500      LINKAGE SECTION.
501      01   customer-ss-no-ls                    PIC 9(9).
502
503      PROCEDURE DIVISION RETURNING customer-ss-no-ls.
504          DISPLAY 'Enter The Customer''s Social Security Number'
505              AT LINE 23 COL 12 ERASE EOS
506          END-DISPLAY
507
508          MOVE SPACES TO switches
509          PERFORM ACCEPT-CUSTOMER-SS-NO
510              UNTIL valid-input OR quit-indicated
511          EXIT METHOD.
512
513      ACCEPT-CUSTOMER-SS-NO.
514          MOVE ZEROS TO customer-ss-no-ls
515          ACCEPT  customer-ss-no-ls AT LINE 12 COL 47
516          IF customer-ss-no-ls NUMERIC
517              MOVE 'YES' TO valid-input-switch
518          ELSE
519              MOVE 'YES' TO valid-input-switch
520              DISPLAY
521                  'Social Security Number not numeric, please re-enter'
522                  AT LINE 23 COL 12 ERASE EOS
523              END-DISPLAY
524              INVOKE Self "DisplayShallWeQuit"
525          END-IF
526
527      END METHOD "InputCustomerSSNo".
528      END CLASS-OBJECT.
529
530      *------Instance Methods ---------------------------------
531
532      OBJECT.
533      OBJECT-STORAGE SECTION.
534      END OBJECT.
535
536      END CLASS CH8CKSCR.
```

CustomerScreen Program

```
*   CH8CUSCR is a class program for CustomerScreen which is a
*    class designed to do all screen I/O for the Customer class.
*      Public Factory Methods are:
*      1. EnterNewCustomer
*      2. DisplayCustomer
*      3. ChangeCustomerName
*      4. RemoveCustomer
*      Private Factory Methods are:
*      1. InputCustomerName
*      2. InputCustomerSSNo
*      3. DisplayShallWeQuit
*      4. DisplayCustomerScreen
*------------------------------------------------------------
```

```
1      CLASS-ID.   CH8CUSCR.
2
3      CLASS-CONTROL.
4          Customer              is class "CH7-CUST".
5
6      CLASS-OBJECT.
7
8      01   switches.
9          05   valid-customer-ss-no-sw    PIC X(3).
10             88   valid-customer-ss-no      VALUE 'YES'.
11         05   valid-customer-name-sw     PIC X(3).
12             88   valid-customer-name       VALUE 'YES'.
13         05   shall-we-quit-sw           PIC X(1).
14             88   valid-input-data    VALUES 'C' 'c' 'S' 's'.
15             88   quit-indicated      VALUES 'S' 's'.
16
17     01   customer-ss-no-ws             PIC X(9).
18     01   customer-name-ws             PIC X(20).
19     01   aCustomer          USAGE IS OBJECT REFERENCE.
20
21     01   return-data-ws.
22         05   return-code-ws              PIC X(3).
23             88   no-record-found    VALUE "NRF".
24             88   duplicate-number   VALUE "DUP".
25             88   other-problem      VALUE "BAD".
26             88   customer-found     VALUE "OK".
27         05   aCustomer-ws      USAGE IS OBJECT REFERENCE.
28
29     *------ Factory Methods ------------------------------------
30
31     *----------------------------------------------------------
32     *  ChangeCustomerName is a CustomerScreen method designed to
33     *    Input & validate Customer SS No & Name and Invoke
34     *    CHangeCustomerName instance method in Customer class
35     *----------------------------------------------------------
36
37      METHOD-ID. "ChangeCustomerName".
38
39      WORKING-STORAGE SECTION.
```

```
40     01   screen-name PIC X(29) VALUE 'CHANGE CUSTOMER NAME SCREEN'.
41
42     PROCEDURE DIVISION.
43         MOVE SPACES TO shall-we-quit-sw
44         PERFORM PROCESS-INPUT
45             UNTIL quit-indicated.
46         EXIT METHOD.
47
48     PROCESS-INPUT.
49         INVOKE Self "DisplayCustomerScreen" USING screen-name
50         END-INVOKE
51         MOVE SPACES TO SWITCHES
52         PERFORM INPUT-CUSTOMER-SS-NO
53             UNTIL quit-indicated OR valid-customer-ss-no
54         PERFORM INPUT-CUSTOMER-NAME
55             UNTIL quit-indicated OR valid-customer-name
56         IF NOT QUIT-INDICATED
57             SET aCustomer TO aCustomer-ws
58             INVOKE aCustomer "ChangeCustomerName"
59                 USING        customer-name-ws, aCustomer
60                 RETURNING    return-data-ws
61             END-INVOKE
62             INVOKE aCustomer "TellCustomerName"
63                 RETURNING customer-name-ws
64             END-INVOKE
65             DISPLAY customer-name-ws AT LINE 15 COL 38
66             DISPLAY 'The Customer Name Has Been Changed.'
67                 AT LINE 23 COL 12 ERASE EOS
68             END-DISPLAY
69             INVOKE Self "DisplayShallWeQuit"
70         END-IF.
71
72     INPUT-CUSTOMER-SS-NO.
73         INVOKE Self "InputCustomerSSNo"
74             RETURNING customer-ss-no-ws
75         END-INVOKE
76
77         IF NOT quit-indicated
78             INVOKE Customer "RetrieveCustomer"
79                 USING        customer-ss-no-ws
80                 RETURNING    return-data-ws
81             END-INVOKE
82             IF no-record-found
83                 PERFORM DISPLAY-NO-CUST-FOUND-MESSAGE
84                 MOVE 'NO'  TO valid-customer-ss-no-sw
85             ELSE
86                 MOVE 'YES' TO valid-customer-ss-no-sw
87             END-IF
88         END-IF.
89
90     INPUT-CUSTOMER-NAME.
91         INVOKE Self "InputCustomerName"
92             RETURNING customer-name-ws
93         END-INVOKE
94         IF NOT quit-indicated
95             MOVE 'YES' TO valid-customer-name-sw
96         END-IF.
```

```
97          DISPLAY-NO-CUST-FOUND-MESSAGE.
98              DISPLAY
99                  'This customer not found, please re-enter SS no'
100                     AT LINE 23 COL 12 ERASE EOS
101             END-DISPLAY
102             INVOKE Self "DisplayShallWeQuit"
103
104         END METHOD "ChangeCustomerName".
105
106         *-------------------------------------------------------------
107         *  DisplayCustomerScreen is a CustomerScreen method designed
108         *    to display the customer screen
109         *-------------------------------------------------------------
110
111         METHOD-ID. "DisplayCustomerScreen".
112
113         LINKAGE SECTION.
114         01  SCREEN-NAME    PIC X(25).
115
116         SCREEN SECTION.
117         01  customer-screen.
118             05   LINE 1  COL 12 VALUE
119                  '*******************************************************'.
120             05   LINE 3  COL 27 VALUE 'Employees'' Credit Union'.
121             05   LINE 5  COL 12 VALUE
122                  '*******************************************************'.
123             05   PIC X(25) FROM SCREEN-NAME LINE 7  COL 26.
124             05   LINE 9  COL 12 VALUE
125                  '*******************************************************'.
126
127             05   LINE 12 COL 23 VALUE
128                     'Social Security Number: _____'.
129             05   LINE 15 COL 23 VALUE
130                     'Customer Name: xxxxxxxxxxxxxxxxxxxx'.
131
132             05   LINE 22 COL 12 VALUE
133                  '*******************************************************'.
134
135         PROCEDURE DIVISION  USING screen-name.
136
137             DISPLAY " " LINE 1 COL 1 ERASE EOS
138             DISPLAY CUSTOMER-SCREEN
139             EXIT METHOD.
140
141         END METHOD "DisplayCustomerScreen".
142
143         *-------------------------------------------------------------
144         *  EnterNewCustomer is a CustomerScreen method designed to input
145         *    and validate customer SS number & name, then Invoke
146         *    CreateNewCustomer instance method in Customer class
147         *-------------------------------------------------------------
148
149         METHOD-ID. "EnterNewCustomer".
150
151         WORKING-STORAGE SECTION.
152
153         01  screen-name PIC X(25) VALUE 'ENTER NEW CUSTOMER SCREEN'.
```

```
154      PROCEDURE DIVISION.
155          MOVE SPACES TO shall-we-quit-sw
156          PERFORM PROCESS-INPUT
157              UNTIL quit-indicated.
158          EXIT METHOD.
159
160      PROCESS-INPUT.
161          INVOKE Self "DisplayCustomerScreen"
162              USING screen-name
163          END-INVOKE
164          MOVE SPACES TO SWITCHES
165          PERFORM INPUT-CUSTOMER-SS-NO
166              UNTIL quit-indicated OR valid-customer-ss-no
167          PERFORM INPUT-CUSTOMER-NAME
168              UNTIL quit-indicated OR valid-customer-name
169          IF NOT QUIT-INDICATED
170              INVOKE Customer "CreateNewCustomer"
171                  USING        customer-ss-no-ws, customer-name-ws
172                  RETURNING    return-data-ws
173              END-INVOKE
174              DISPLAY SPACE AT LINE 23 COL 12 ERASE EOL
175              INVOKE Self "DisplayShallWeQuit"
176          END-IF.
177
178      INPUT-CUSTOMER-SS-NO.
179          INVOKE Self "InputCustomerSSNo"
180              RETURNING customer-ss-no-ws
181          END-INVOKE
182
183          IF NOT quit-indicated
184              INVOKE Customer "RetrieveCustomer"
185                  USING        customer-ss-no-ws
186                  RETURNING    return-data-ws
187              END-INVOKE
188              IF no-record-found
189                  MOVE 'YES' TO valid-customer-ss-no-sw
190              ELSE
191                  MOVE 'NO' TO valid-customer-ss-no-sw
192                  DISPLAY
193                  'Duplicate SS Number found, please re-enter'
194                      AT LINE 23 COL 12 ERASE EOS
195                  END-DISPLAY
196                  INVOKE Self "DisplayShallWeQuit"
197              END-IF
198          END-IF.
199
200      INPUT-CUSTOMER-NAME.
201          INVOKE Self "InputCustomerName"
202              RETURNING customer-name-ws
203          END-INVOKE
204          IF NOT quit-indicated
205              MOVE 'YES' TO valid-customer-name-sw
206          END-IF.
207
208      END METHOD "EnterNewCustomer".
209
210      *-------------------------------------------------------------
```

```
211        *  DisplayCustomer is a CustomerScreen method designed to
212        *     Input customer-ss-no,  Invoke RetrieveCustomer method
213        *       in Customer class, and display customer name
214        *---------------------------------------------------------
215
216         METHOD-ID. "DisplayCustomer".
217
218         WORKING-STORAGE SECTION.
219         01   screen-name      PIC X(25) VALUE '  DISPLAY CUSTOMER INFO '.
220
221
222         PROCEDURE DIVISION.
223             MOVE SPACES TO shall-we-quit-sw
224             PERFORM PROCESS-INPUT
225                 UNTIL quit-indicated.
226             EXIT METHOD.
227
228         PROCESS-INPUT.
229             INVOKE Self "DisplayCustomerScreen"
230                 USING screen-name
231             END-INVOKE
232             MOVE SPACES TO SWITCHES
233             PERFORM INPUT-CUSTOMER-SS-NO
234                 UNTIL quit-indicated OR valid-customer-ss-no
235
236             IF NOT QUIT-INDICATED
237                 INVOKE aCustomer-ws "TellCustomerName"
238                     RETURNING customer-name-ws
239                 END-INVOKE
240                 DISPLAY customer-name-ws AT LINE 15 COL 38
241                 DISPLAY SPACE AT LINE 23 COL 12 ERASE EOL
242                 INVOKE Self "DisplayShallWeQuit"
243             END-IF.
244
245         INPUT-CUSTOMER-SS-NO.
246             INVOKE Self "InputCustomerSSNo"
247                 RETURNING customer-ss-no-ws
248             END-INVOKE
249
250             IF NOT quit-indicated
251                 INVOKE Customer "RetrieveCustomer"
252                     USING         customer-ss-no-ws
253                     RETURNING    return-data-ws
254                 END-INVOKE
255                 IF no-record-found
256                     PERFORM DISPLAY-NO-CUST-FOUND-MESSAGE
257                     MOVE 'NO'  TO valid-customer-ss-no-sw
258                 ELSE
259                     MOVE 'YES' TO valid-customer-ss-no-sw
260                 END-IF
261             END-IF.
262
263         DISPLAY-NO-CUST-FOUND-MESSAGE.
264             DISPLAY
265                 'This customer not found, please re-enter SS no'
266                     AT LINE 23 COL 12 ERASE EOS
267             END-DISPLAY
```

```
268             INVOKE Self "DisplayShallWeQuit"
269
270        END METHOD "DisplayCustomer".
271
272        *------------------------------------------------------------
273        *  InputCustomerName is a CustomerScreen method designed
274        *    to input & validate customer name
275        *------------------------------------------------------------
276
277        METHOD-ID. "InputCustomerName".
278
279        LINKAGE SECTION.
280        01   customer-name-ls              PIC X(20).
281             88 customer-name-missing    VALUE SPACES.
282
283
284
285        PROCEDURE DIVISION RETURNING customer-name-ls.
286           DISPLAY
287               'Message: Enter The Customer''s Name'
288                LINE 23 COL 12 ERASE EOS
289           END-DISPLAY
290
291           MOVE SPACES TO switches
292           PERFORM ACCEPT-CUSTOMER-NAME
293               UNTIL valid-customer-name OR quit-indicated
294
295           EXIT METHOD.
296
297        ACCEPT-CUSTOMER-NAME.
298           MOVE SPACES TO customer-name-ls
299           DISPLAY customer-name-ls AT LINE 15 COL 38
300           DISPLAY
301               'Message: Enter The Customer''s Name'  AT LINE 23 COL 12
302                   ERASE EOS
303           ACCEPT customer-name-ls AT LINE 15 COL 38
304           IF customer-name-missing
305               DISPLAY 'Customer Name is Missing, Please Enter'
306                   AT LINE 23 COL 12 ERASE EOS
307               END-DISPLAY
308               INVOKE Self "DisplayShallWeQuit"
309           ELSE
310               MOVE 'YES' to valid-customer-name-sw
311           END-IF
312
313        END METHOD "InputCustomerName".
314
315        *------------------------------------------------------------
316        *  InputCustomerSSNo is a CustomerScreen method designed to
317        *    input and validate customer-ss-no
318        *------------------------------------------------------------
319
320        METHOD-ID. "InputCustomerSSNo".
321
322        LINKAGE SECTION.
323        01   customer-ss-no-ls             PIC X(9).
324
```

```
325          PROCEDURE DIVISION RETURNING customer-ss-no-ls.
326              DISPLAY
327                  'Message: Enter The Customer''s Social Security Number'
328                      LINE 23 COL 12 ERASE EOS
329              END-DISPLAY
330
331              MOVE SPACES TO valid-customer-ss-no-sw
332                            shall-we-quit-sw
333              PERFORM ACCEPT-CUSTOMER-SS-NO
334                  UNTIL valid-customer-ss-no OR quit-indicated
335              EXIT METHOD.
336
337          ACCEPT-CUSTOMER-SS-NO.
338              MOVE SPACES TO customer-ss-no-ls
339              DISPLAY customer-ss-no-ls AT LINE 12 COL 47
340              ACCEPT  customer-ss-no-ls AT LINE 12 COL 47.
341              IF customer-ss-no-ls NUMERIC
342                  MOVE 'YES' TO valid-customer-ss-no-sw
343              ELSE
344                  DISPLAY
345                      'Social Security Number not numeric, please re-enter'
346                      AT LINE 23 COL 12 ERASE EOS
347                  END-DISPLAY
348                  INVOKE Self "DisplayShallWeQuit"
349              END-IF
350
351          END METHOD "InputCustomerSSNo".
352
353          *------------------------------------------------------------
354          *   RemoveCustomer is a CustomerScreen method designed to
355          *      Input and validate customer ss number, then
356          *      Invoke RemoveCustomer instance method in Customer Class
357          *------------------------------------------------------------
358
359          METHOD-ID. "RemoveCustomer".
360
361          WORKING-STORAGE SECTION.
362
363          01   screen-name PIC X(25) VALUE 'REMOVE CUSTOMER SCREEN'.
364
365          PROCEDURE DIVISION.
366              MOVE SPACES TO shall-we-quit-sw
367              PERFORM PROCESS-INPUT
368                  UNTIL quit-indicated.
369              EXIT METHOD.
370
371          PROCESS-INPUT.
372              INVOKE Self "DisplayCustomerScreen"
373                  USING screen-name
374              END-INVOKE
375              MOVE SPACES TO SWITCHES
376              PERFORM INPUT-CUSTOMER-SS-NO
377                  UNTIL quit-indicated OR valid-customer-ss-no
378              IF NOT QUIT-INDICATED
379                  SET aCustomer to aCustomer-ws
380                  INVOKE aCustomer "TellCustomerName"
381                      RETURNING   customer-name-ws
```

```
382               END-INVOKE
383               DISPLAY customer-name-ws AT LINE 15 COL 38 ERASE EOL
384
385               DISPLAY 'Do You Want to Remove this Customer?'
386                   AT LINE 23 COL 12 ERASE EOS
387               INVOKE Self "DisplayShallWeQuit"
388               IF NOT QUIT-INDICATED
389                   INVOKE aCustomer "RemoveCustomer"
390                       USING        aCustomer
391                       RETURNING    return-data-ws
392                   DISPLAY 'This Customer has been Removed'
393                       AT LINE 23 COL 12 ERASE EOS
394               ELSE
395                   DISPLAY 'This Customer has NOT been Removed'
396                       AT LINE 23 COL 12 ERASE EOS
397               END-IF
398               INVOKE Self "DisplayShallWeQuit"
399           END-IF.
400
401       INPUT-CUSTOMER-SS-NO.
402           INVOKE Self "InputCustomerSSNo"
403               RETURNING customer-ss-no-ws
404           END-INVOKE
405
406           IF NOT quit-indicated
407               INVOKE Customer "RetrieveCustomer"
408                   USING        customer-ss-no-ws
409                   RETURNING    return-data-ws
410               END-INVOKE
411               IF no-record-found
412                   MOVE 'NO'  TO valid-customer-ss-no-sw
413                   PERFORM DISPLAY-NO-CUST-FOUND-MESSAGE
414               ELSE
415                   MOVE 'YES' TO valid-customer-ss-no-sw
416               END-IF
417           END-IF.
418
419       DISPLAY-NO-CUST-FOUND-MESSAGE.
420           DISPLAY
421               'This customer not found, please re-enter SS no'
422                   AT LINE 23 COL 12 ERASE EOS
423           END-DISPLAY
424           INVOKE Self "DisplayShallWeQuit"
425
426       END METHOD "RemoveCustomer".
427
428       *-------------------------------------------------------------
429       *  DisplayShallWeQuit is a CustomerScreen method designed
430       *     to display a 'Should We Quit Message'
431       *     and accept the response
432       *-------------------------------------------------------------
433
434       METHOD-ID. "DisplayShallWeQuit".
435
436       PROCEDURE DIVISION.
437
438           MOVE SPACES TO shall-we-quit-sw
```

```
439             PERFORM UNTIL VALID-INPUT-DATA
440                 DISPLAY "              Enter C to Continue, S to Stop: _"
441                     AT LINE 24 COL 12 ERASE EOS
442                     ACCEPT shall-we-quit-sw LINE 24 COL 55
443             END-PERFORM.
444
445         END METHOD "DisplayShallWeQuit".
446         END CLASS-OBJECT.
447
448        *------Instance Methods -------------------------------------
449
450         OBJECT.
451         OBJECT-STORAGE SECTION.
452         END OBJECT.
453
454         END CLASS CH8CUSCR.
```

CHAPTER 9:

Object COBOL and Beyond

Previous chapters have dealt with object-oriented concepts and Object COBOL development. This final chapter will briefly recap what has been covered and then take a quick look into the future—the future of OO development and Object COBOL.

By now you have developed a good understanding of the basics of object-oriented systems development using Object COBOL. We want to emphasize, however, that the material presented here has dealt only with the basics. There are numerous OO-related concepts and Object COBOL topics that we have either omitted or not covered in sufficient detail. In this chapter, we want to mention some of these omissions and suggest sources for additional reading.

Finally, many organizations are concerned about how to implement OO. Although the many benefits are becoming obvious, the path to OO is not well marked. Should the transition be a gradual, incremental evolutionary process, or, as some advocate, should the shift be more rapid and revolutionary? We discuss this issue briefly in the following section.

Moving to OO Development

If you've made it this far in the book, then it is obvious that you've made a commitment to object technology. But how will companies make the move to object development? Will it be a drastic change wherein the IS departments switch all development efforts to the object paradigm (i.e., a *revolutionary approach*)? Or will it be a gradual move in which IS departments slowly adopt object development through new projects and the eventual migration of existing systems (i.e., the *evolutionary approach)*? The answer is going to depend on the company, its past development projects, its current development projects, its dedication to development, and so on. We feel that Object COBOL will be an important development tool for companies moving to object development.

Object COBOL offers the opportunity for companies that want to gradually move to object development. Object COBOL provides a familiar environment to the 3 million existing COBOL programmers. Object COBOL code is also compatible with the billions of lines of existing COBOL code. However, the migration to object development is much more than the programming language used—the entire development environment must be considered. One possible way to migrate to object development is to integrate the concepts of objects with traditional techniques (such as structured development).

The integration of object and traditional techniques can help smooth the path to object development. This integration can be accomplished in several ways. For example, classes can be derived from the output of traditional techniques (such as data flow diagrams and entity-relationship diagrams). The idea is that entity-relationship diagrams can provide the classes; the data flow diagrams provide the processing methods; and object interaction diagrams provide the dynamic behavior of classes.

Another way is to introduce object concepts into a familiar environment. For example, the object-oriented structured design (OOSD) technique supports structured design notation. Thus, a design could gradually shift from traditional techniques to object development. Several authors have indicated that many of the techniques currently used are closely related to the new concepts of objects. Jackson Structured Development and Information Engineering, which are considered data-oriented, are conceptually only slightly different from object development, thus providing a possible migratory path.

Finally, the move to object development is not restricted to new development. The migration can begin with existing systems and "work backwards" (i.e., existing systems can gradually be modified to include object components). One popular technique, called *object wrapping*, involves covering traditional programs with an interface (i.e., using our previously described interface classes layer from the Class Layer model). Gradually, when changes become necessary, the programs are changed totally to class programs.

Wrapping is a transitional step and can save development time and money by preventing the reinvention of existing applications. Techniques such as wrapping allow for incremental *redevelopment* and provide an economically justifiable migration to object development. One plan to migrate to total object development, as developed and implemented at AT&T, is to gradually introduce object techniques into the life cycle, starting at OOP and working backwards through the life cycle to requirements analysis.

Object development represents a different paradigm from traditional techniques. Thus, the move to completely adopt the object approach is very costly in personnel costs. It has been suggested that training time is typically 6 to 18 months for object developers; it takes 2 to 8 months for an experienced programmer to become productive using an OOP language. The evolutionary approach can relieve some of the immediate need to be fully trained. Instead, the developers can 'ease' into object development over a period of time without a total loss of productivity. Object COBOL provides a good way for existing developers to ease into object development.

A Brief Review of Where We Have Been

We began by introducing first OO concepts and then Object COBOL. We initially developed a simple class program in Chapter 5 and then invoked methods residing in the class.

Chapter 5 also introduced the concept of layered systems design, as shown again in Figure 9.1. Chapter 6 illustrated the use of inherited methods in superclasses and subclasses.

Both Chapters 5 and 6 described the design and construction of problem domain classes for the credit union system. At the end of Chapter 6, we developed class programs for <u>Account</u>, <u>CheckingAccount</u>, <u>LoanAccount</u>, and <u>SavingsAccount</u>.

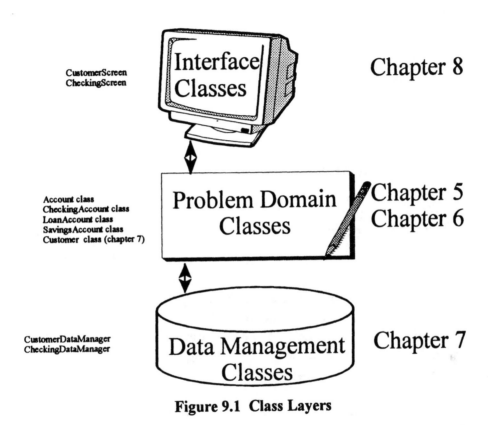

Figure 9.1 Class Layers

Chapter 7 turned to the design of data management classes. Persistent instance storage was accomplished with the development of two data management classes: <u>CheckingDataManager</u> and <u>CustomerDataManager</u>. We then developed user interface class programs in Chapter 8. <u>MenuScreen</u>, <u>CheckingScreen</u>, and <u>CustomerScreen</u> classes were written, and their use was demonstrated.

The complete object model for the credit union system is shown in Figure 9.2. During the development of the system, we continuously emphasized and demonstrated the benefits of layered design and OO development. We saw that although we significantly expanded the system, modifications to the existing class programs were either not necessary or, at worst, minor and localized.

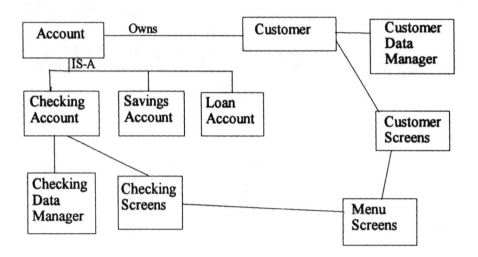

Figure 9.2   Credit Union System Object Model

ADDITIONAL READING

Here we have concentrated on OO programming using Object COBOL. Although we dealt with object models and object interaction diagrams, our primary interest was in developing class programs using Object COBOL. We therefore neglected OO analysis and design concepts and tools. OO analysis and design are important topics, and you will want to study them as you continue learning about OO. Several excellent OO analysis and design books have been published. We have listed several of these in the bibliographies at the end of the chapters throughout the book, and encourage you to explore them.

In contrast to the many OO analysis and design books, very few Object COBOL texts have been issued. (This was one reason why we decided to write this book.) Five of the more recent comprehensive texts (indicated in boldface) are listed in the bibliography at the end of this chapter. The Arranga and Coyle book, in particular, deals in some depth with topics we have intentionally omitted, such as collections. Again, you are encouraged to examine these and other books to further your knowledge of OO.

KEY TERMS

Evolutionary approach   **Redevelopment**
Object wrapping   **Revolutionary approach**

REVIEW QUESTIONS

1. How can Object COBOL facilitate the move to OO development by organizations?

2. What strategies can companies use to make the transition to OO development?

3. How can OO techniques and traditional techniques be integrated?

EXERCISE

1. Find a company (locally or discussed in the literature) that is using OO development techniques. What strategy did the company use to make the transition to OO—evolutionary or revolutionary? How successful was the transition?

BIBLIOGRAPHY

Arranga, E., and Coyle, F. Object-Oriented COBOL. SIGS Publications, 1996.

Booch, G. Object-Oriented Analysis and Design with Applications. Benjamin-Cummings, 1994.

Brown, D. An Introduction to Object-Oriented Analysis. John Wiley & Sons, 1997.

Chapin, N. Standard Object-Oriented COBOL. John Wiley & Sons, 1997.

Coad. P. Object Models: Strategies, Patterns, and Applications. Prentice-Hall, 1995.

Coad, P., and Yourdon, E. Object-Oriented Analysis. Yourdon Press, Prentice-Hall, 1991.

Fichman, R. G., and Kemerer, C. F. "Object-oriented and Conventional Analysis and Design Methodologies" IEEE Computer. 25 (10), October 1992: 22–39.

Firesmith, D. G., Object-Oriented Requirements Analysis and Logical Design. John Wiley & Sons, 1993.

Jacobson, I., et al. Object-Oriented Software Engineering: A Use Case Driven Approach. Addison-Wesley, 1992.

Jacobson, I., and Lindstrom, F. "Re-engineering of Old Systems to an Object-Oriented Architecture" SIGPLAN Notices. 26 (11), 1991: 340–350.

Jeffcoate, J., and Wesely, I. Objects in Use: Meeting Business Needs. Ovum, Ltd, 1992.

Kamath, Y. H., Smiian, R. E., and Smith, J. G. "Reaping Benefits with Object-Oriented Technology" AT&T Technical Journal. 72 (5), October 1993: 14–24.

Levey, R. Re-Engineering COBOL with Objects. McGraw-Hill, 1995.

Martin, J. and Odell, J. Object-Oriented Analysis and Design. Prentice-Hall, 1992.

Moad, J. "Cultural Barriers Slow Reusability" Datamation. 35 (22), 1989, 87–92.

Montgomery, S. L. Object-Oriented Information Engineering: Analysis, Design, and Implementation. AP Professional, 1994.

Obin, R. Object-Orientation: An Introduction for COBOL Programmers. 2nd ed., Micro Focus Publishing, 1995.

Price, W. **Elements of Object-Oriented COBOL. Object-Z Publishing, 1997.**

Rabin, S. "Transitioning Information Systems COBOL Developers into Object COBOL Technicians" Object Magazine, January 1995, pp. 71–75.

Rumbaugh, J., et al. Object-Oriented Modeling and Design. Prentice-Hall, 1991.

Satzinger, J, and Orvik, T. Object-Oriented Approach: Concepts, Modeling, and Systems Development. Boyd & Fraser, 1996.

Scholtz, J., Chidamber, S., Glass, R., Goerner, A., Rosson, M. B., Stark, M., and Vessey, I. "Object-Oriented Programming: The Promise and the Reality" Journal of Systems and Software. 23 (2), November 1993: 199–204.

Shlaer, S. and Mellor, S. J. Object Lifecycles: Modeling the World in States. Prentice-Hall, 1992.

Shumate, K. "Structured Analysis and Object-Oriented Design Are Compatible" Ada Letters. 11 (4), May/June 1991, 78–90.

Sully, P. Modeling the World with Objects. New York: Prentice-Hall, 1993.

Sutcliffe, A. G. "Object-oriented Systems Development: Survey of Structured Methods" Information and Software Technology. 33 (6), July/August 1991, 433–442.

Taylor, D. A. Object-Oriented Systems: Planning and Implementation. John Wiley & Sons, 1992.

Taylor, D. A. Object-Oriented Technology: A Manager's Guide. Addison-Wesley, 1990.

Topper, A. **Object-Oriented Development in COBOL. McGraw-Hill, 1995.**

Yourdon, E. Object-Oriented Systems Design: An Integrated Approach. Yourdon Press, Prentice-Hall, 1994.

Wasserman, A. I., Pircher, P. A., and Muller, R. J. "The Object-Oriented Structured Design Notation for Software Design Representation" IEEE Computer. 23 (3), March 1990: 50–63.

INDEX